New Modern Farmhouse Floor Plans 2023

Where Classic Meets Contemporary

Chris Cruz

Copyright © 2023 **Chris Cruz**

All rights reserved. This book or any portion thereof may not be reproduced or used in any manner whatsoever without the express written permission of the publisher except for the use of brief quotations in a book review

Contents

Introduction 1

CHAPTER ONE: The Black Creek 3 Farmhouse floor plan 2

CHAPTER TWO: The Ponderosa 2 Farmhouse Floor Plans 4

CHAPTER THREE: The Black Creek 2 Farmhouse Floor Plans 7

CHAPTER FOUR: The Peachtree 2 Farmhouse Floor Plans 10

CHAPTER FIVE: The River Oaks Farmhouse Floor Plans 12

CHAPTER SIX: The Oxford Farmhouse Floor Plans 14

CHAPTER SEVEN: The Tumbleweed Farmhouse Floor Plans 17

CHAPTER EIGHT: The Shady Oaks Farmhouse Floor Plans 19

CHAPTER NINE: The River Bend Farmhouse Floor Plans 22

CHAPTER TEN: The Cedar Point Farmhouse Floor Plans 24

CHAPTER ELEVEN: The Rock Creek Farmhouse Floor Plans 26

CHAPTER TWELVE: The Peach Tree Farmhouse Floor Plans 30

CHAPTER THIRTEEN: The Shadowcrest Farmhouse Floor Plans 34

CHAPTER FOURTEEN: The Sage Farmhouse Floor Plans 37

CHAPTER FIFTEEN: The Hidden Point Farmhouse Floor Plans 39

CHAPTER SIXTEEN: The Caymus Farmhouse Floor Plans 41

CHAPTER SEVENTEEN: The Windsor Creek Farmhouse Floor Plans 44

CHAPTER EIGHTEEN: The Valley View Farmhouse Floor Plans 48

CHAPTER NINETEEN: The Daisey Farmhouse floor plans 52

CHAPTER TWENTY: The Merry Oaks Farmhouse Floor plans 55

CHAPTER TWENTY-ONE: The Spring Bluff Farmhouse floor plan 57

CHAPTER TWENTY-TWO: The Blackberry Farmhouse floor plan 59

CHAPTER TWENTY-THREE: The Honeysuckle Farmhouse floor plan 61

CHAPTER TWENTY-FOUR: The Mulberry Farmhouse floor plans 63

CHAPTER TWENTY-FIVE: The Aspen Hill 65

CHAPTER TWENTY-SEVEN: The Indian Trail Farmhouse floor plan 71

CHAPTER TWENTY-EIGHT: The Sandy Ridge Farmhouse floor plan 73

CHAPTER TWENTY-NINE: The Cherry Grove Farmhouse floor plan 77

CHAPTER THIRTY: The Cotton Grove Farmhouse floor plan 80

Introduction

Modern farmhouse floor plans have become increasingly popular in recent years, as they offer a perfect blend of traditional farmhouse design with modern elements, resulting in a unique and appealing architectural style. Characterized by clean lines, simple shapes, and a combination of materials such as wood, metal, and stone, this design trend has captured the attention of homeowners and builders alike.

The modern farmhouse style emphasizes comfort, simplicity, practicality, and functionality, making it suitable for all types of lifestyles, whether in the city or the countryside. Inspired by the classic American farmhouse, which was once the center of life for rural families, modern farmhouse floor plans seek to create a warm and welcoming environment that is both functional and aesthetically pleasing.

The layout of modern farmhouse floor plans typically emphasizes openness, with a large living area that flows into the kitchen and dining area. Bedrooms are often located on the second floor, with a large master suite that includes a spacious bathroom and walk-in closet. This design feature promotes a sense of intimacy and privacy, while also providing ample space for family and guests.

Another hallmark of modern farmhouse floor plans is the integration of outdoor living spaces, such as porches, patios, and balconies. These areas provide a relaxing atmosphere where one can enjoy the fresh air and beautiful views, enhancing the overall livability of the home.

Natural materials, such as wood, stone, and brick, are also a prominent feature of modern farmhouse design. These materials add warmth and character to the home, providing a timeless aesthetic that will never go out of style. Overall, modern farmhouse floor plans are an excellent choice for those seeking a comfortable, functional, and aesthetically pleasing home design.

CHAPTER ONE: The Black Creek 3 Farmhouse floor plan

House Plan Features

- Bedrooms: 3
- Bathrooms: 2.5
- Main Ceiling Height: 10'
- Main Roof Pitch: 9 ON 12

Plan Details in Square Footage

- Living Square Feet: 2291
- Total Square Feet: 4496
- Porch Square Feet: 739
- Bonus Room Square Feet: 603

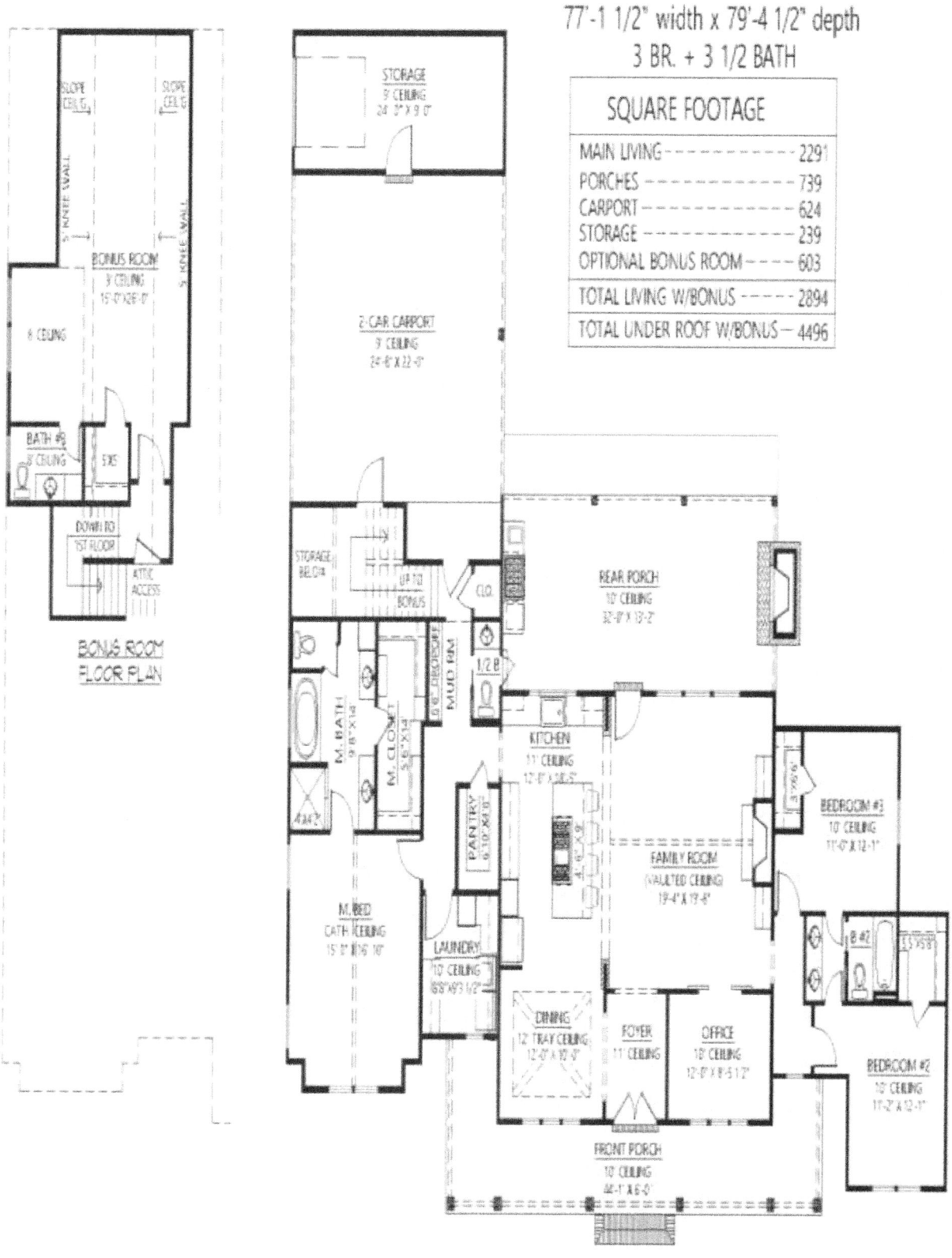

CHAPTER TWO: The Ponderosa 2 Farmhouse Floor Plans

House Plan Features

- Bedrooms: 4
- Bathrooms: 3.5
- Garage Bays: 3
- Main Ceiling Height: 10'
- Main Roof Pitch: 10 ON 12

Plan Details in Square Footage

- Living Square Feet: 2514
- Total Square Feet: 4180
- Porch Square Feet: 766
- Garage Square Feet: 900

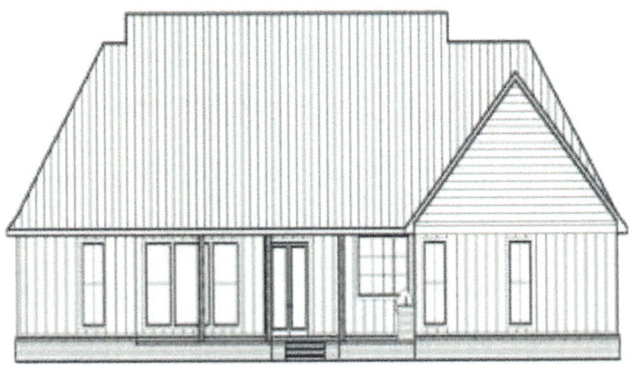

Ponderosa 2

85'-10" width x 65'-8" depth
4 BDRM / 3 1/2 BATH

SQUARE FOOTAGE	
LIVING	2514
PORCHES	766
GARAGE/STORAGE	900
TOTAL UNDER ROOF	4180

CHAPTER THREE: The Black Creek 2 Farmhouse Floor Plans

House Plan Features

- Bedrooms: 4
- Bathrooms: 3.5

Plan Details in Square Footage

- Living Square Feet: 2841
- Total Square Feet: 5264
- Porch Square Feet: 862
- Garage Square Feet: 878
- Bonus Room Square Feet: 683

The Black Creek 2

79'-0" width x 80'-5 1/2" depth
4 BR. + 3 1/2 BATH

SQUARE FOOTAGE	
MAIN LIVING	2841
FRONT PORCH	362
REAR PORCH	500
GARAGE	878
OPTIONAL BONUS ROOM	683
TOTAL LIVING W/BONUS	3524
TOTAL UNDER ROOF W/BONUS	5264

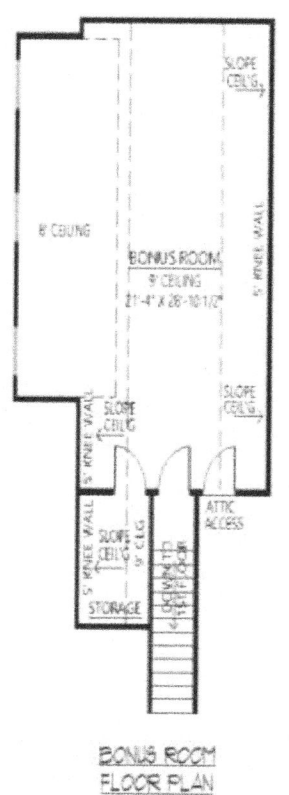

BONUS ROOM FLOOR PLAN

CHAPTER FOUR: The Peachtree 2 Farmhouse Floor Plans

House Plan Features

- Bedrooms: 4
- Bathrooms: 2.5
- Garage Bays: 2
- Main Ceiling Height: 10'
- Main Roof Pitch: 9 ON 12

Plan Details in Square Footage

- Living Square Feet: 1985
- Total Square Feet: 3488
- Porch Square Feet: 471
- Garage Square Feet: 641
- Bonus Room Square Feet: 391

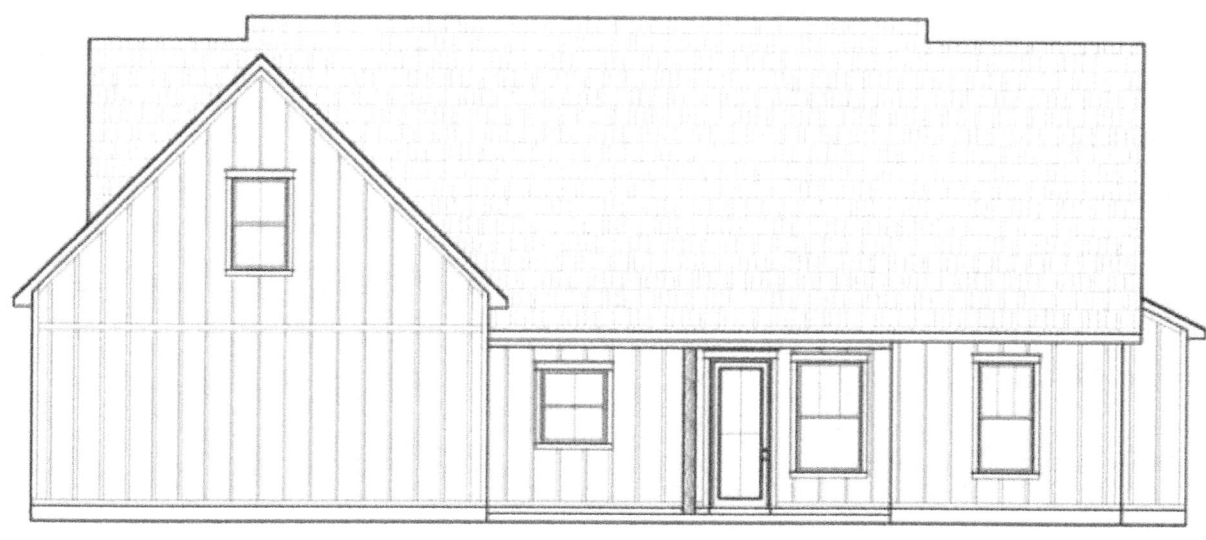

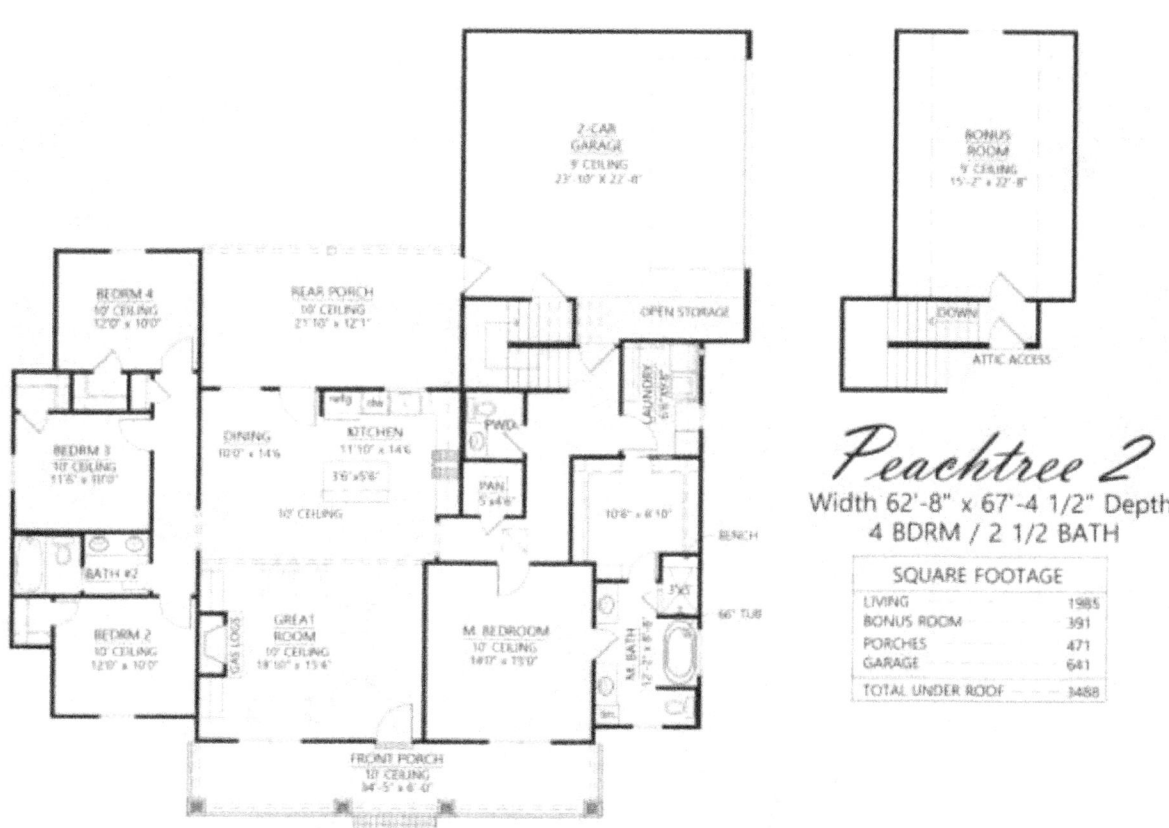

Peachtree 2
Width 62'-8" x 67'-4 1/2" Depth
4 BDRM / 2 1/2 BATH

SQUARE FOOTAGE	
LIVING	1985
BONUS ROOM	391
PORCHES	471
GARAGE	641
TOTAL UNDER ROOF	3488

CHAPTER FIVE: The River Oaks Farmhouse Floor Plans

House Plan Features

- Bedrooms: 4
- Bathrooms: 2
- Garage Bays: 2
- Main Ceiling Height: 10'
- Main Roof Pitch: 9 ON 12

Plan Details in Square Footage

- Living Square Feet: 1843
- Total Square Feet: 3026
- Garage Square Feet: 574

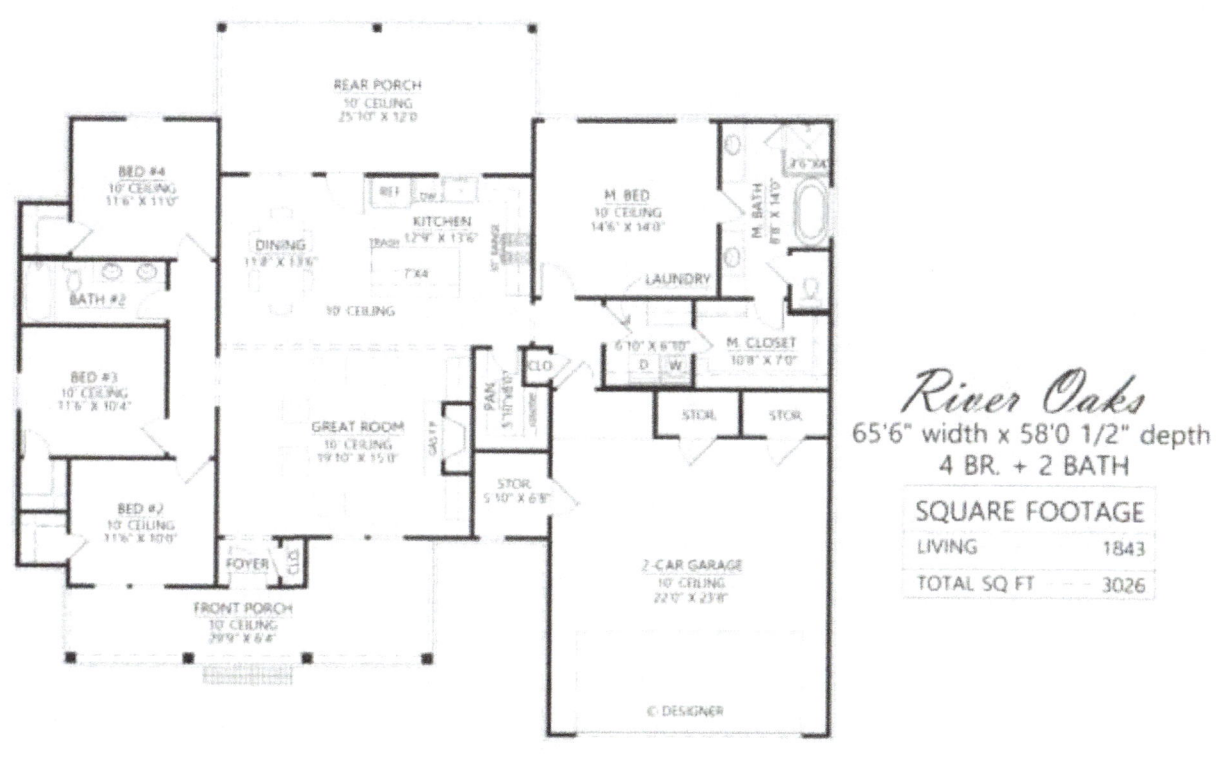

River Oaks
65'6" width x 58'0 1/2" depth
4 BR. + 2 BATH

SQUARE FOOTAGE	
LIVING	1843
TOTAL SQ FT	3026

CHAPTER SIX: The Oxford Farmhouse Floor Plans

House Plan Features

- Bedrooms: 4
- Bathrooms: 3.5
- Garage Bays: 3
- Main Ceiling Height: 10'
- Main Roof Pitch: 9 on 12

Plan Details in Square Footage

- Living Square Feet: 3346
- Total Square Feet: 6472
- Porch Square Feet: 1308
- Garage Square Feet: 1034
- Bonus Room Square Feet: 734

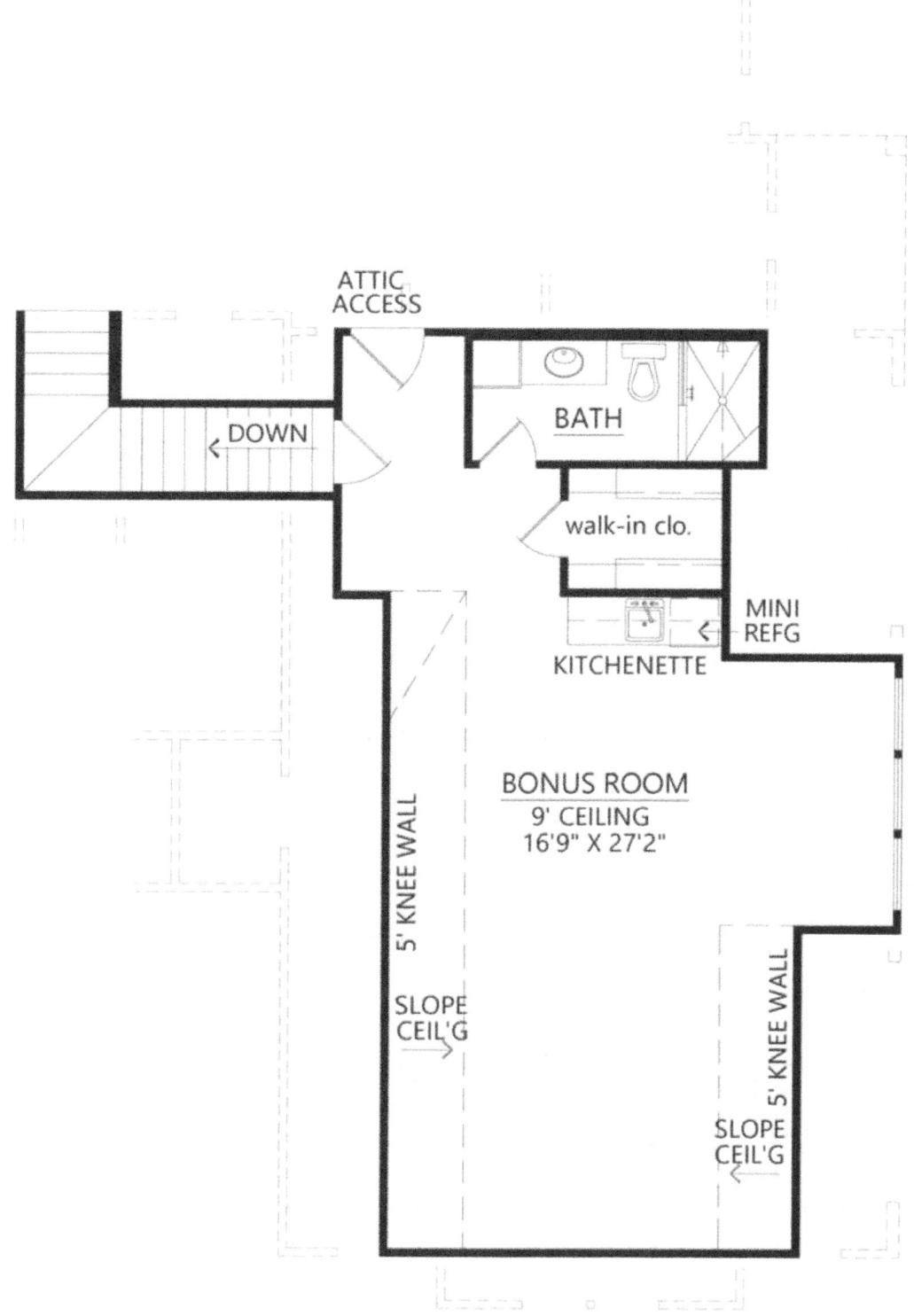

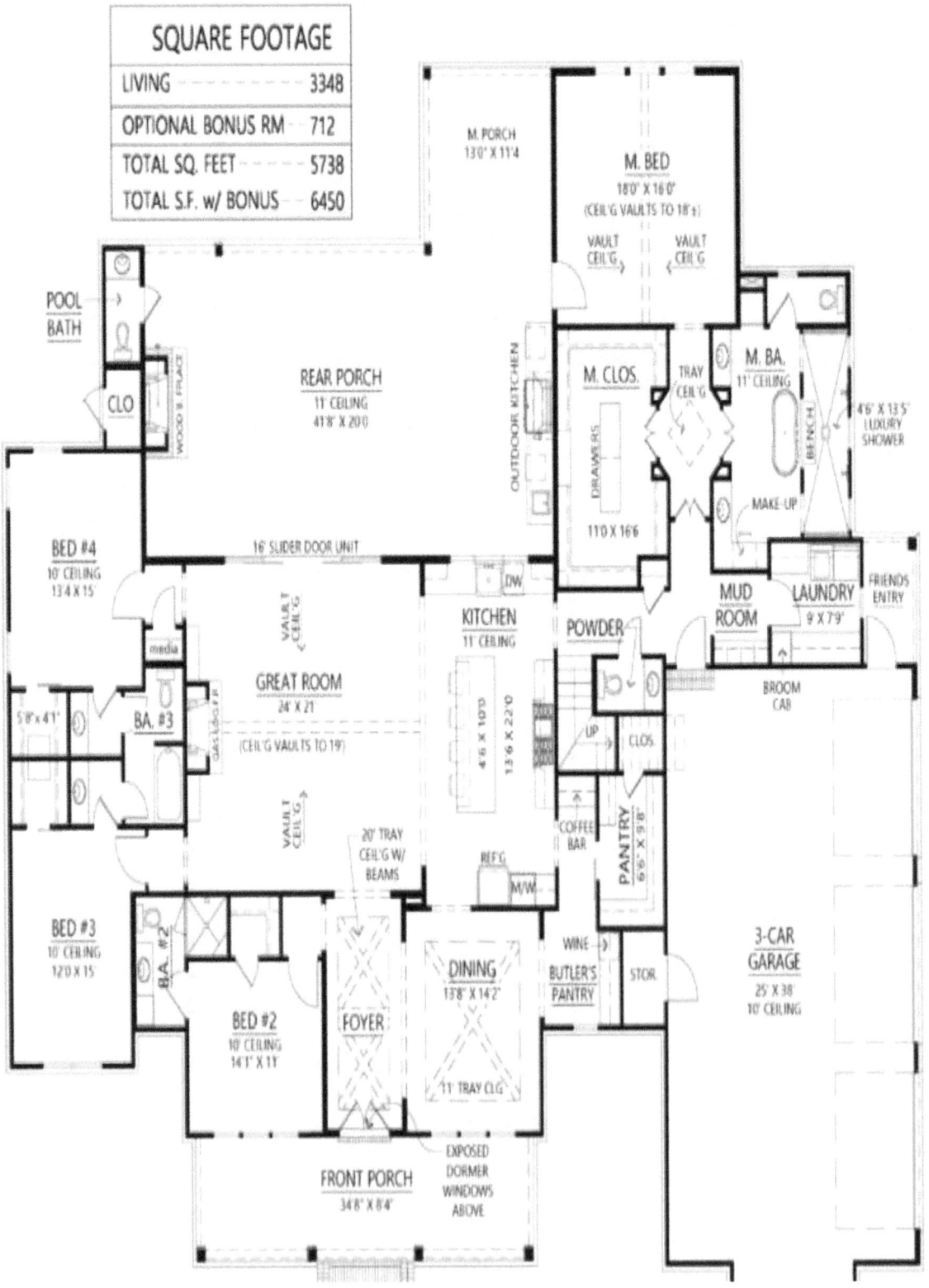

CHAPTER SEVEN: The Tumbleweed Farmhouse Floor Plans

House Plan Features

- Bedrooms: 3
- Bathrooms: 2
- Garage Bays: 2
- Main Ceiling Height: 10'
- Main Roof Pitch: 9 on 12

Plan Details in Square Footage

- Living Square Feet: 1818
- Total Square Feet: 2673
- Porch Square Feet: 236
- Garage Square Feet: 621

REAR ELEVATION

The Tumbleweed

65'2" width x 48'7 1/2" depth
3 BDRM / 2 BATH
W/ HOME OFFICE

SQUARE FOOTAGE	
LIVING	1818
PORCHES	233
GARAGE	621
TOTAL UNDER ROOF	2672

CHAPTER EIGHT: The Shady Oaks Farmhouse Floor Plans

House Plan Features

- Bedrooms: 4
- Bathrooms: 2
- Garage Bays: 2
- Main Ceiling Height: 10'
- Main Roof Pitch: 9 on 12

Plan Details in Square Footage

- Living Square Feet: 2291
- Total Square Feet: 3501
- Porch Square Feet: 659
- Garage Square Feet: 551

CHAPTER NINE: The River Bend Farmhouse Floor Plans

House Plan Features

- Bedrooms: 3
- Bathrooms: 2
- Garage Bays: 2
- Main Ceiling Height: 10'
- Main Roof Pitch: 9 on 12

Plan Details in Square Footage

- Living Square Feet: 1973
- Total Square Feet: 2978
- Porch Square Feet: 425
- Garage Square Feet: 580

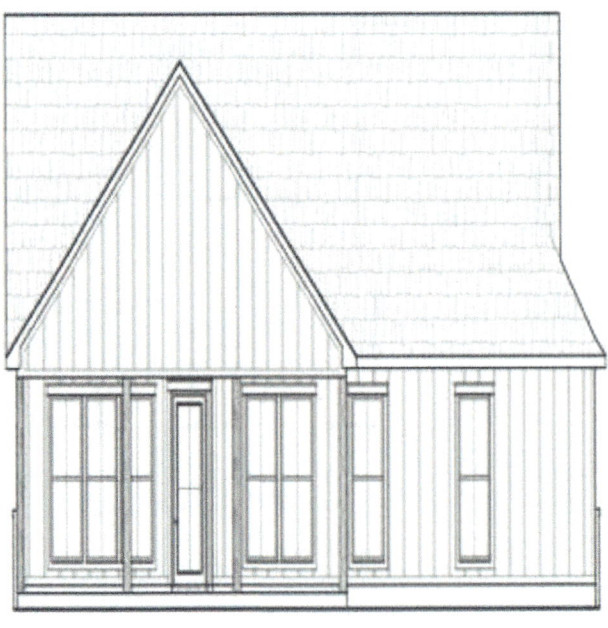

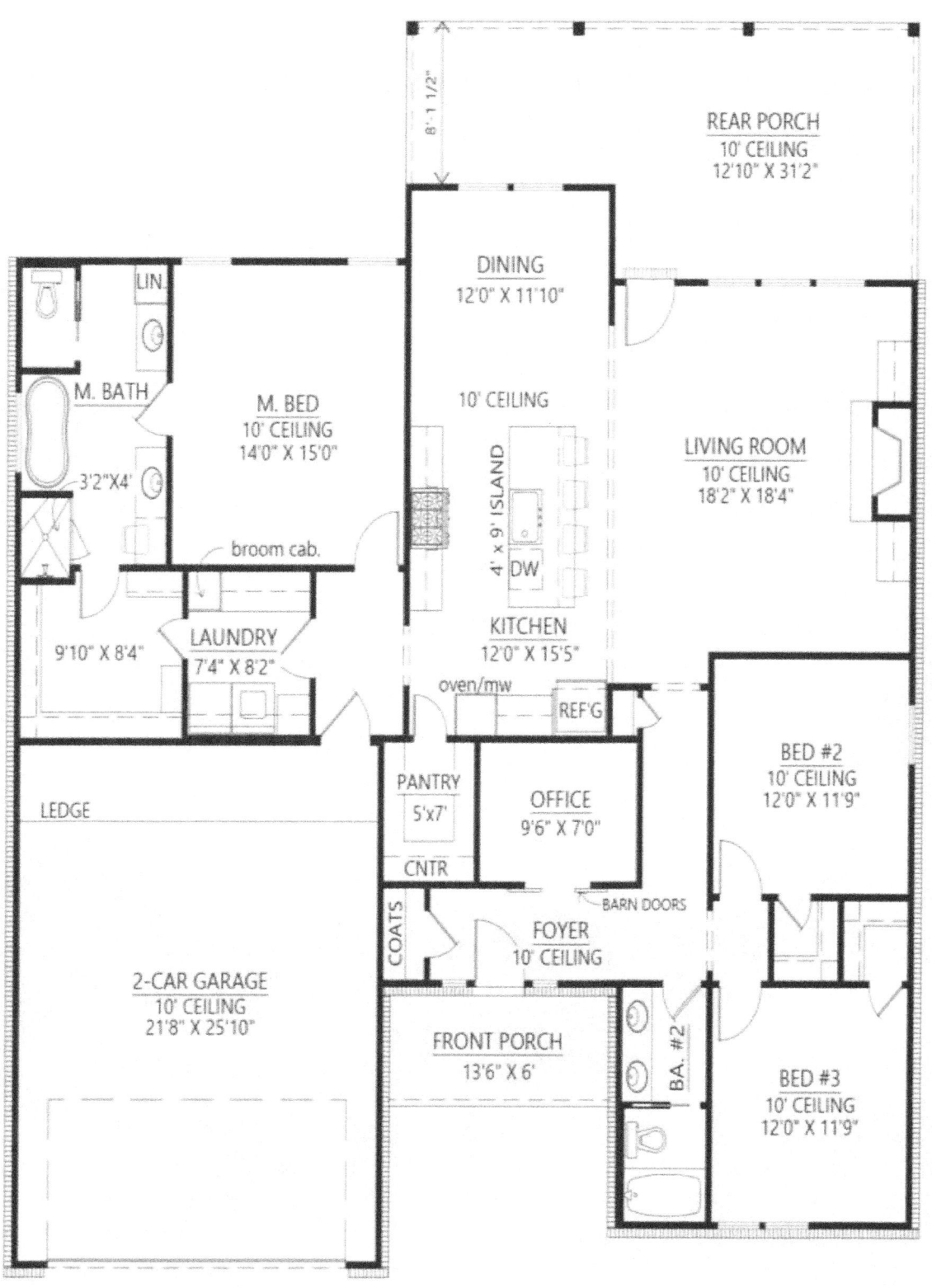

CHAPTER TEN: The Cedar Point Farmhouse Floor Plans

House Plan Features

- Bedrooms: 4
- Bathrooms: 2.5

Plan Details in Square Footage

- Living Square Feet: 2098
- Total Square Feet: 3315
- Porch Square Feet: 501
- Garage Square Feet: 573

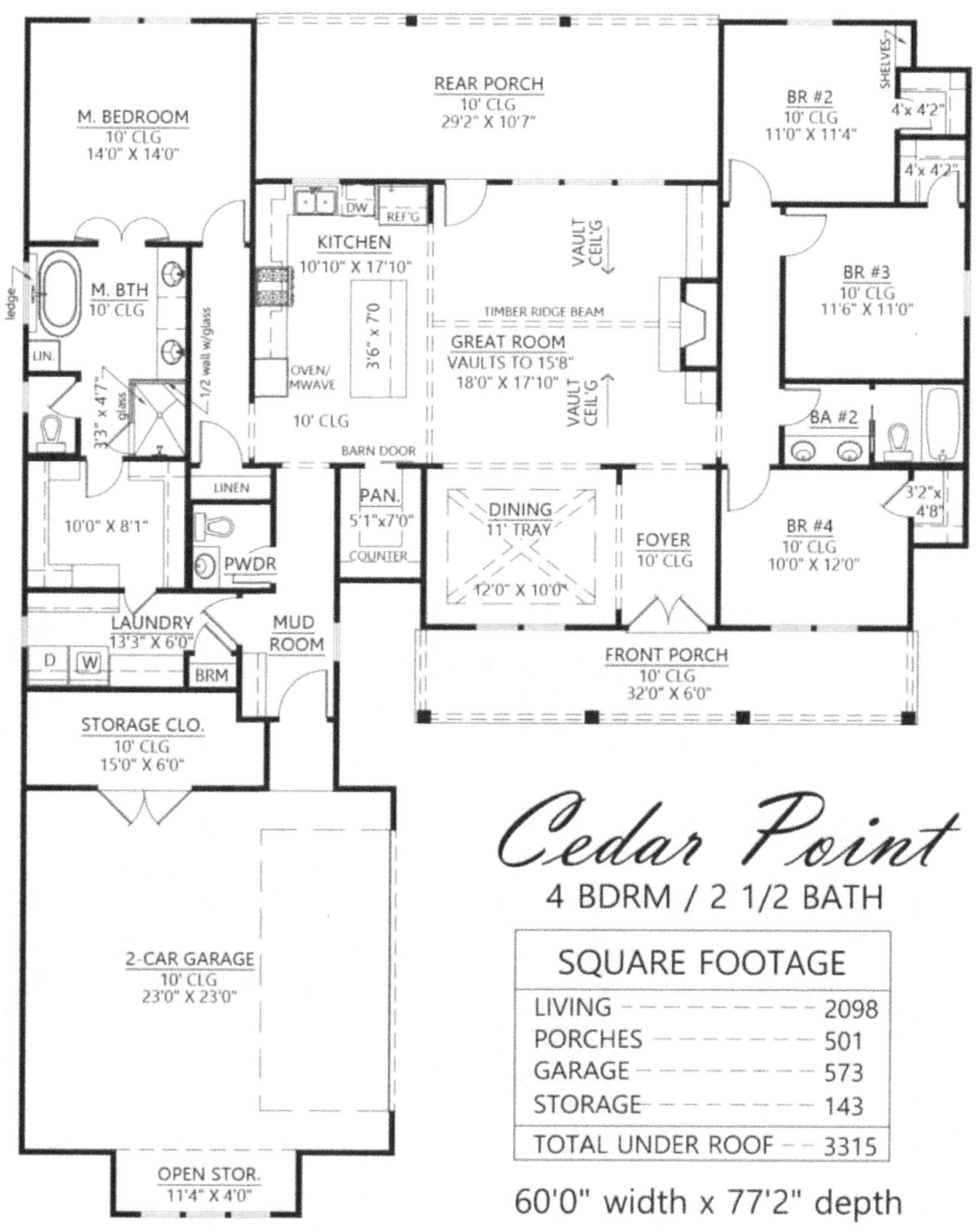

Cedar Point

4 BDRM / 2 1/2 BATH

SQUARE FOOTAGE	
LIVING	2098
PORCHES	501
GARAGE	573
STORAGE	143
TOTAL UNDER ROOF	3315

60'0" width x 77'2" depth

CHAPTER ELEVEN: The Rock Creek Farmhouse Floor Plans

House Plan Features

- Bedrooms: 4
- Bathrooms: 4.5
- Garage Bays: 6
- Main Roof Pitch: 9 on 12

Plan Details in Square Footage

- Living Square Feet: 3127
- Total Square Feet: 6240
- Porch Square Feet: 1420
- Garage Square Feet: 995
- Bonus Room Square Feet: 700

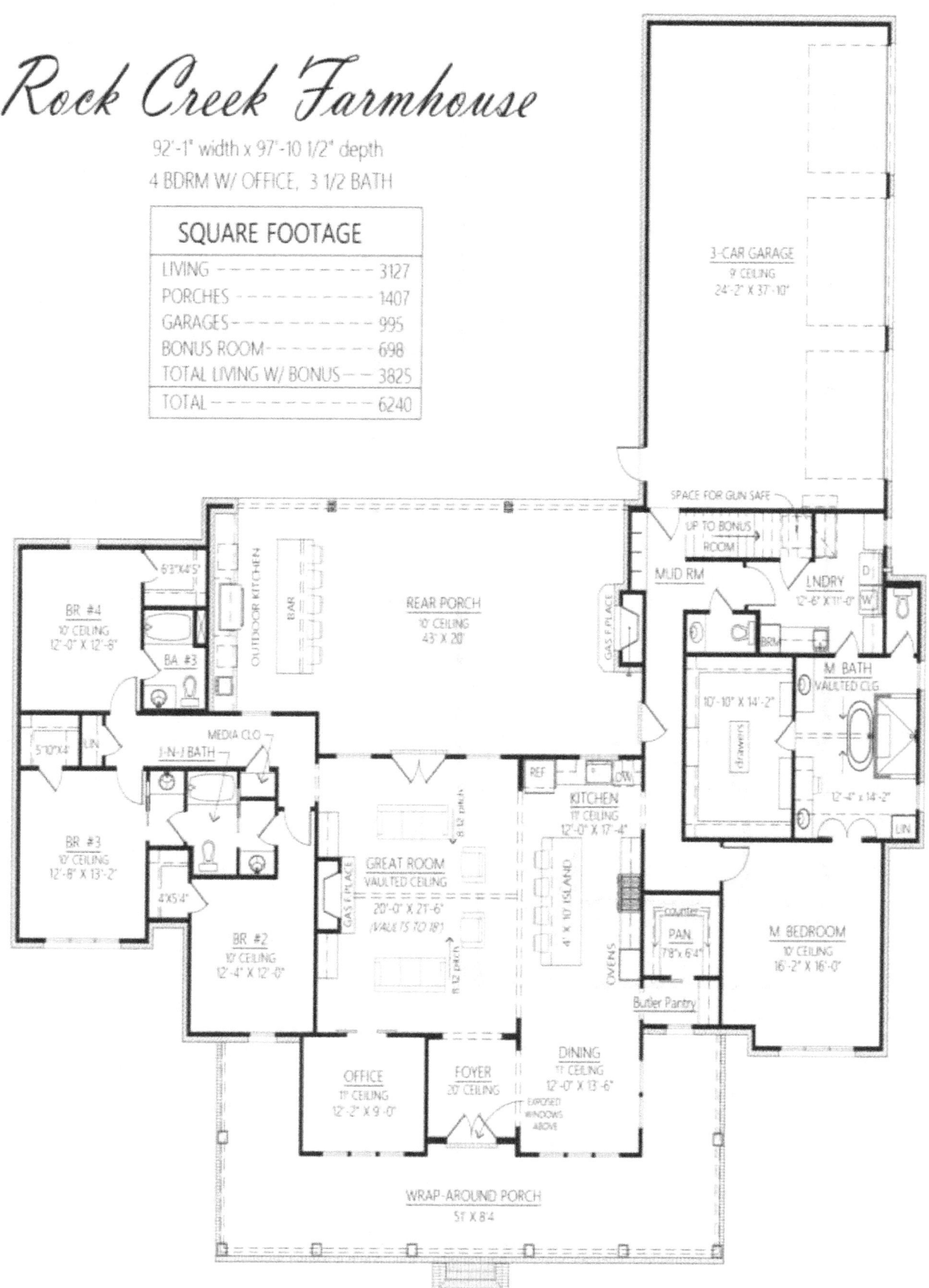

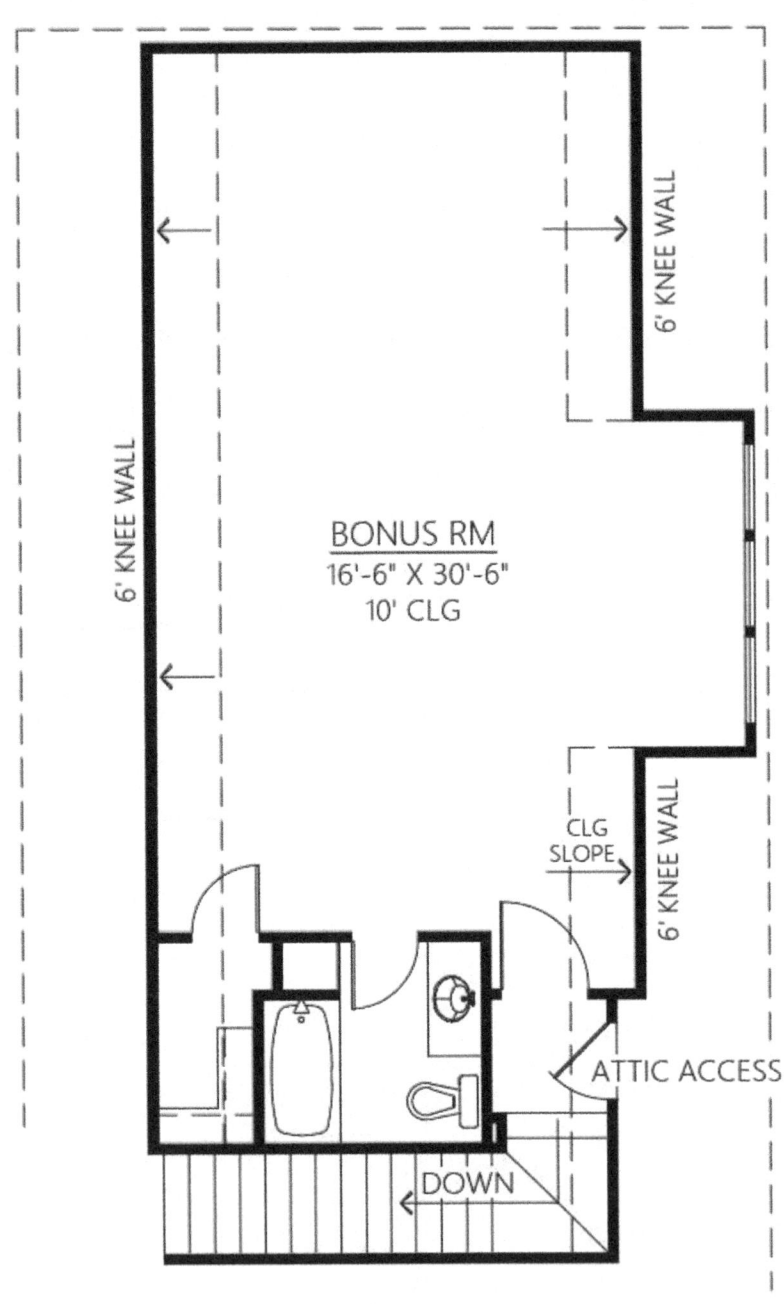

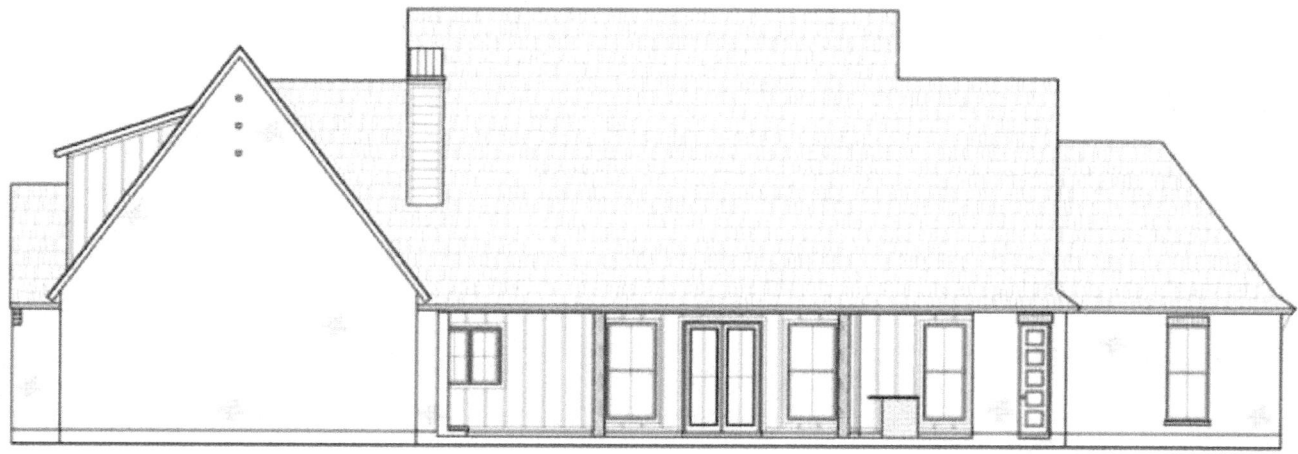

REAR ELEVATION

CHAPTER TWELVE: The Peach Tree Farmhouse Floor Plans

House Plan Features

- Bedrooms: 4
- Bathrooms: 2.5
- Garage Bays: 4
- Main Ceiling Height: 10'
- Main Roof Pitch: 9 on 12

Plan Details in Square Footage

- Living Square Feet: 1880
- Total Square Feet: 2929
- Porch Square Feet: 472
- Garage Square Feet: 578

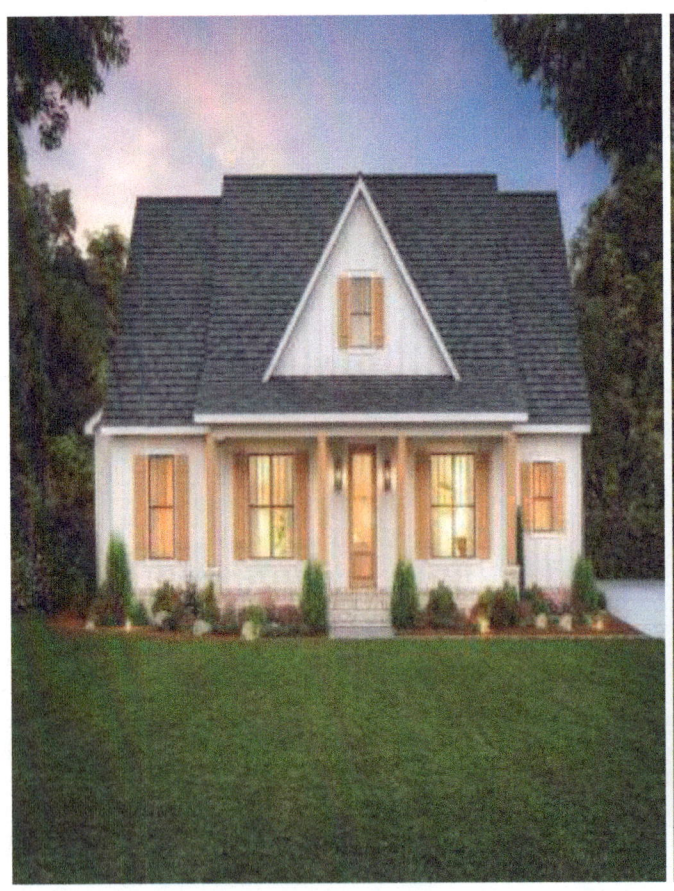

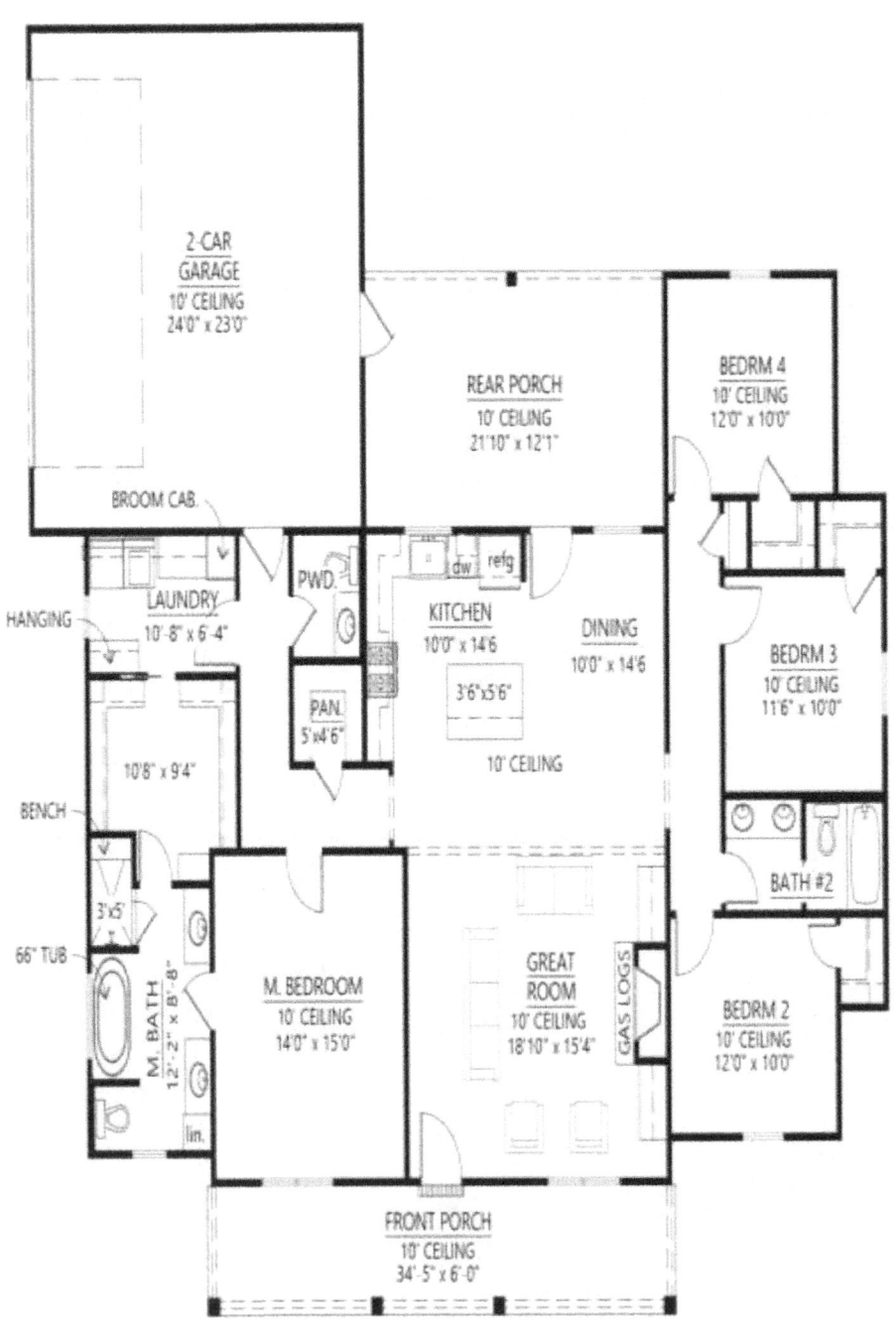

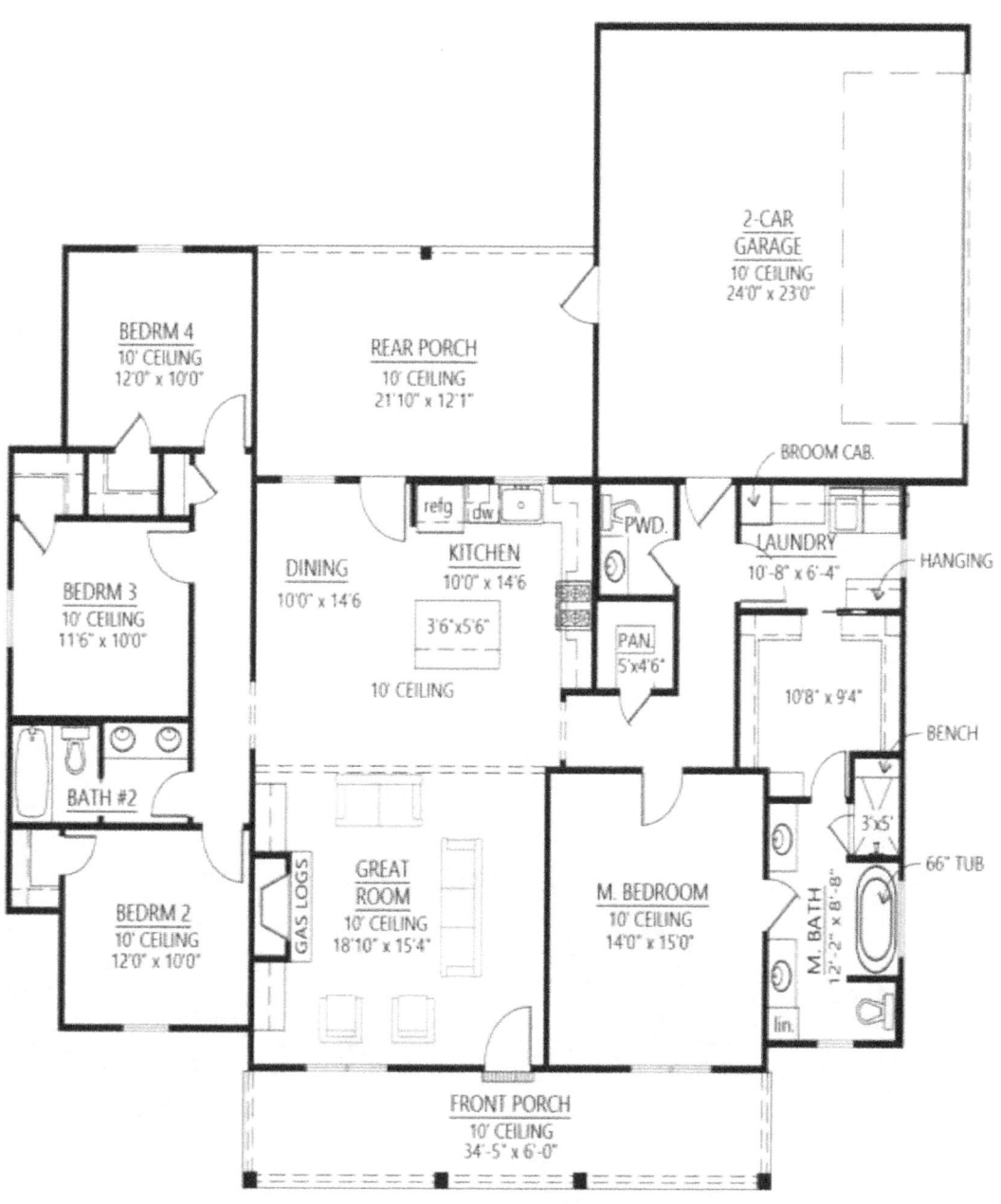

CHAPTER THIRTEEN: The Shadowcrest Farmhouse Floor Plans

House Plan Features

- Bedrooms: 3
- Bathrooms: 2
- Garage Bays: 2
- Main Ceiling Height: 9'
- Main Roof Pitch: 9 on 12

Plan Details in Square Footage

- Living Square Feet: 1600
- Total Square Feet: 2684
- Porch Square Feet: 454
- Garage Square Feet: 578

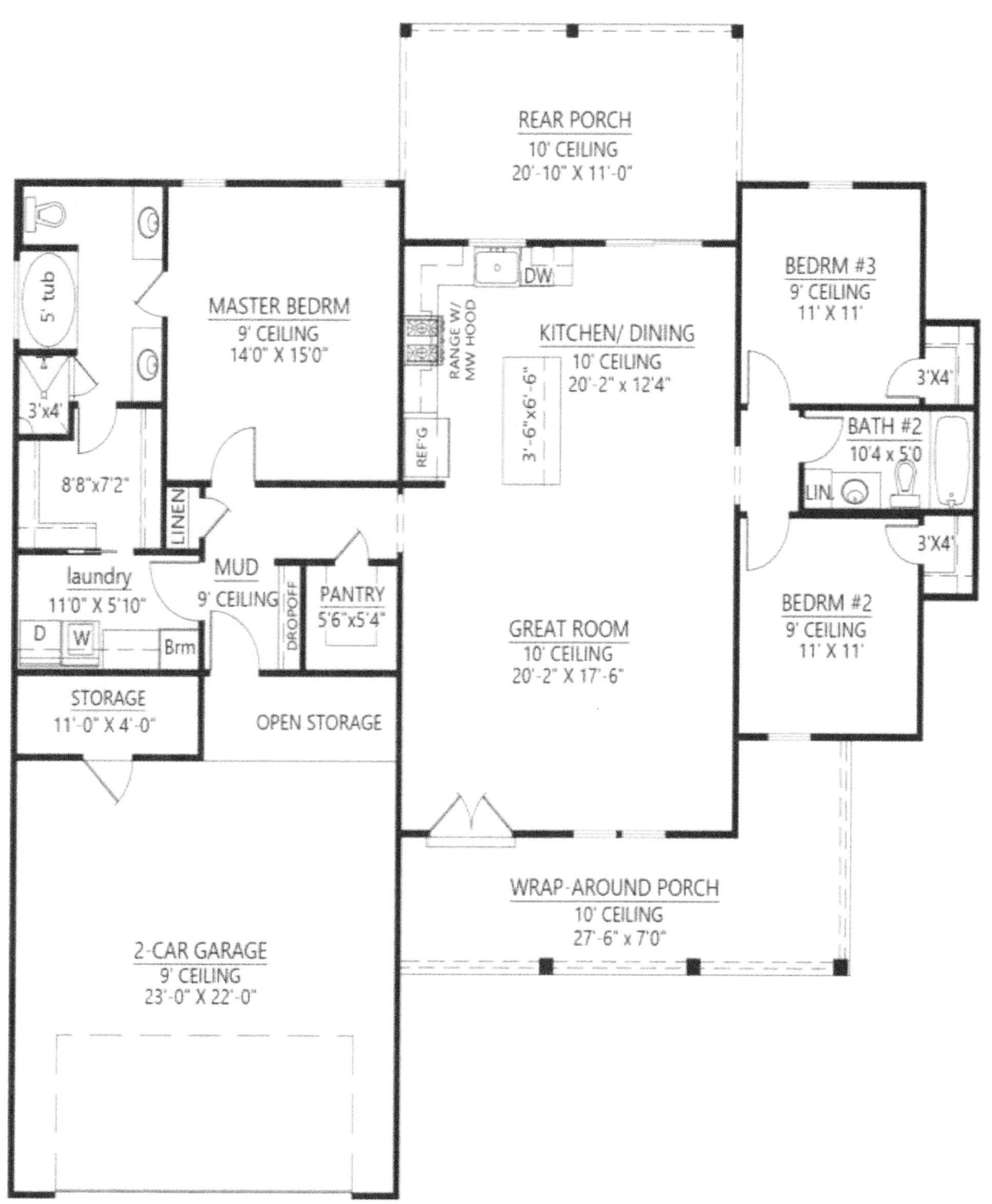

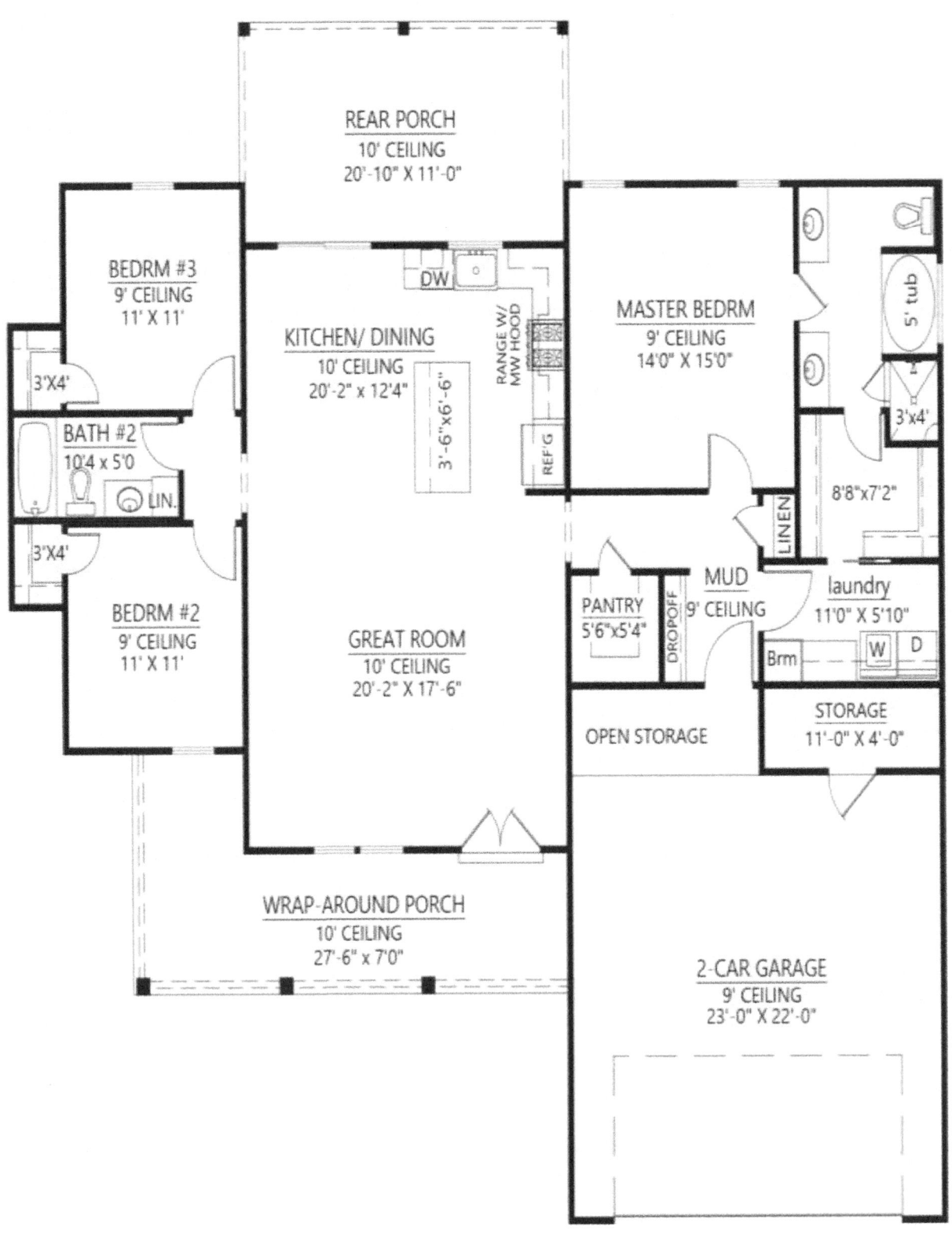

CHAPTER FOURTEEN: The Sage Farmhouse Floor Plans

House Plan Features

- Bedrooms: 3
- Bathrooms: 2.5
- Garage Bays: 2
- Main Ceiling Height: 10'
- Main Roof Pitch: 9 on 12

Plan Details in Square Footage

- Living Square Feet: 1993
- Total Square Feet: 2987
- Porch Square Feet: 404
- Garage Square Feet: 587

Sage Farmhouse

72'-8" width x 60'-9" depth

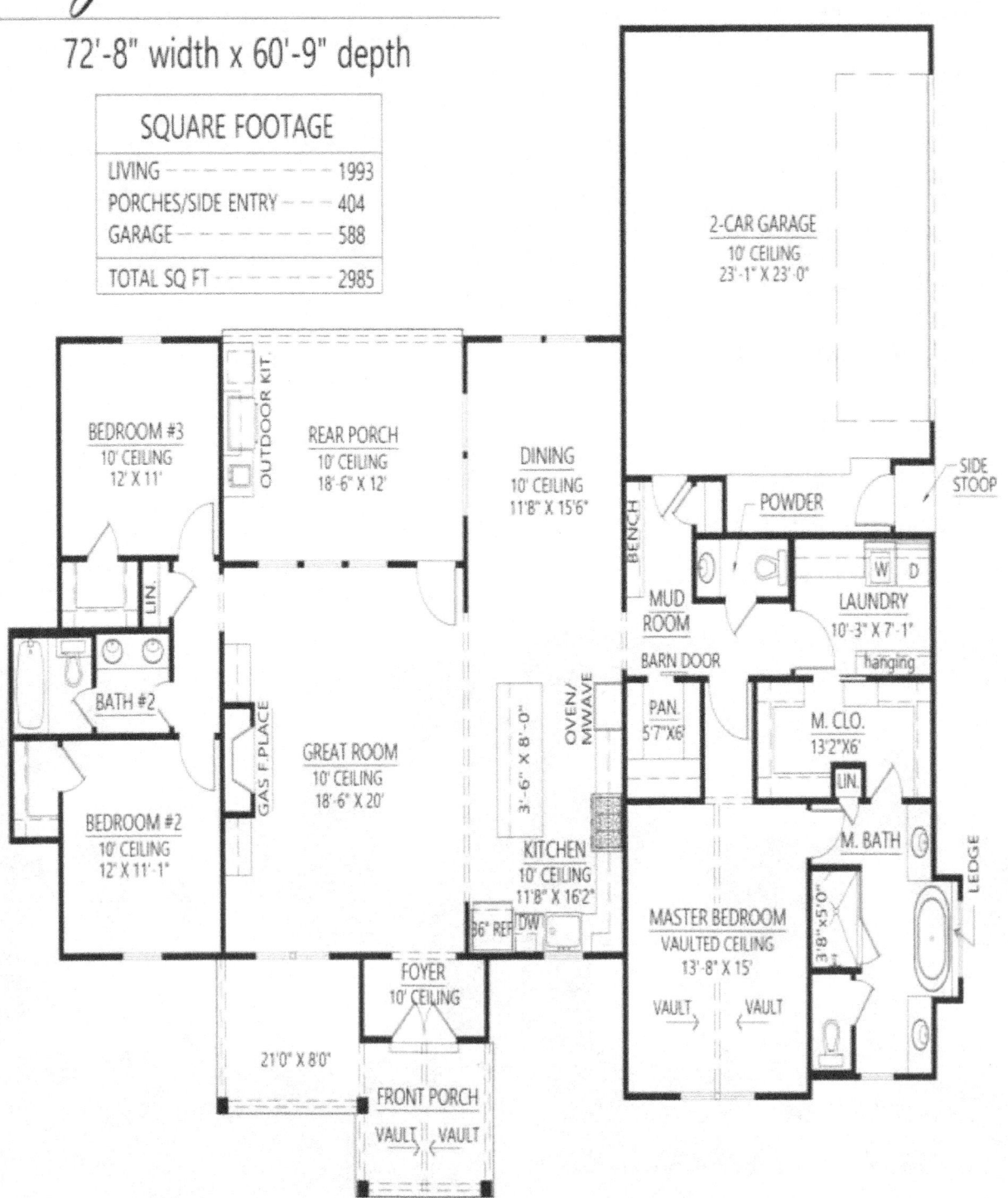

CHAPTER FIFTEEN: The Hidden Point Farmhouse Floor Plans

House Plan Features

- Bedrooms: 3
- Bathrooms: 2
- Garage Bays: 2
- Main Ceiling Height: 10'
- Main Roof Pitch: 9 on 12

Plan Details in Square Footage

- Living Square Feet: 1941
- Total Square Feet: 2967
- Porch Square Feet: 464
- Garage Square Feet: 562

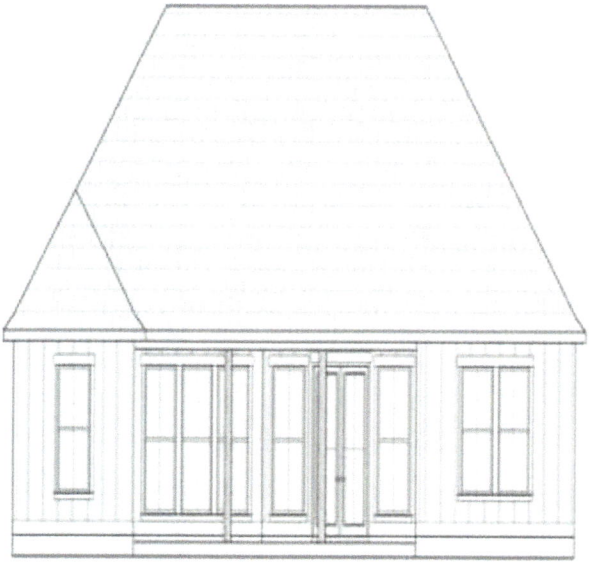

REAR ELEVATION

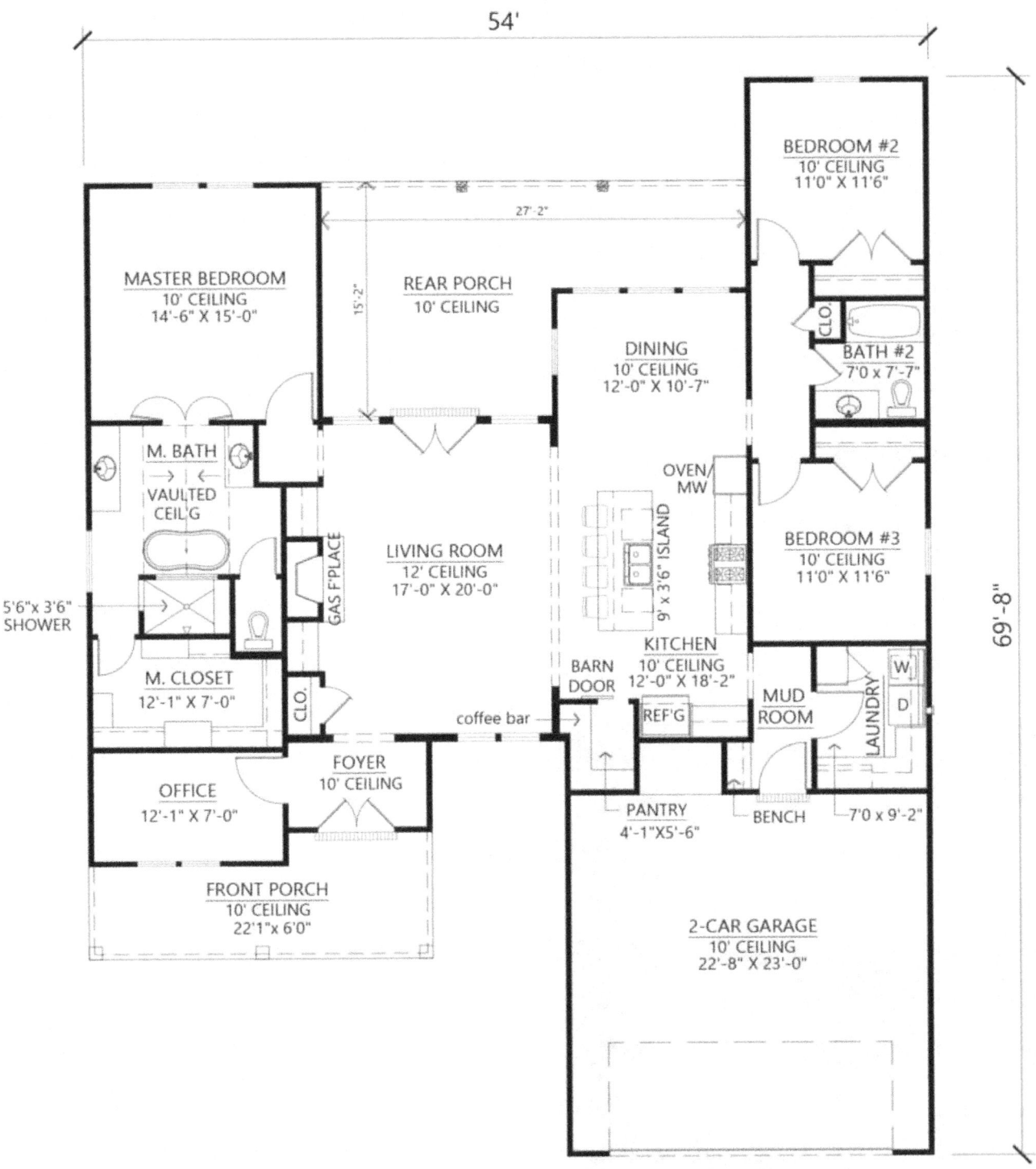

CHAPTER SIXTEEN: The Caymus Farmhouse Floor Plans

House Plan Features

- Bedrooms: 4
- Bathrooms: 3.5
- Garage Bays: 3
- Main Ceiling Height: 10'
- Main Roof Pitch: 9 on 12

Plan Details in Square Footage

- Living Square Feet: 3449
- Total Square Feet: 5677
- Porch Square Feet: 1216
- Garage Square Feet: 1015
- Bonus Room Square Feet: 462

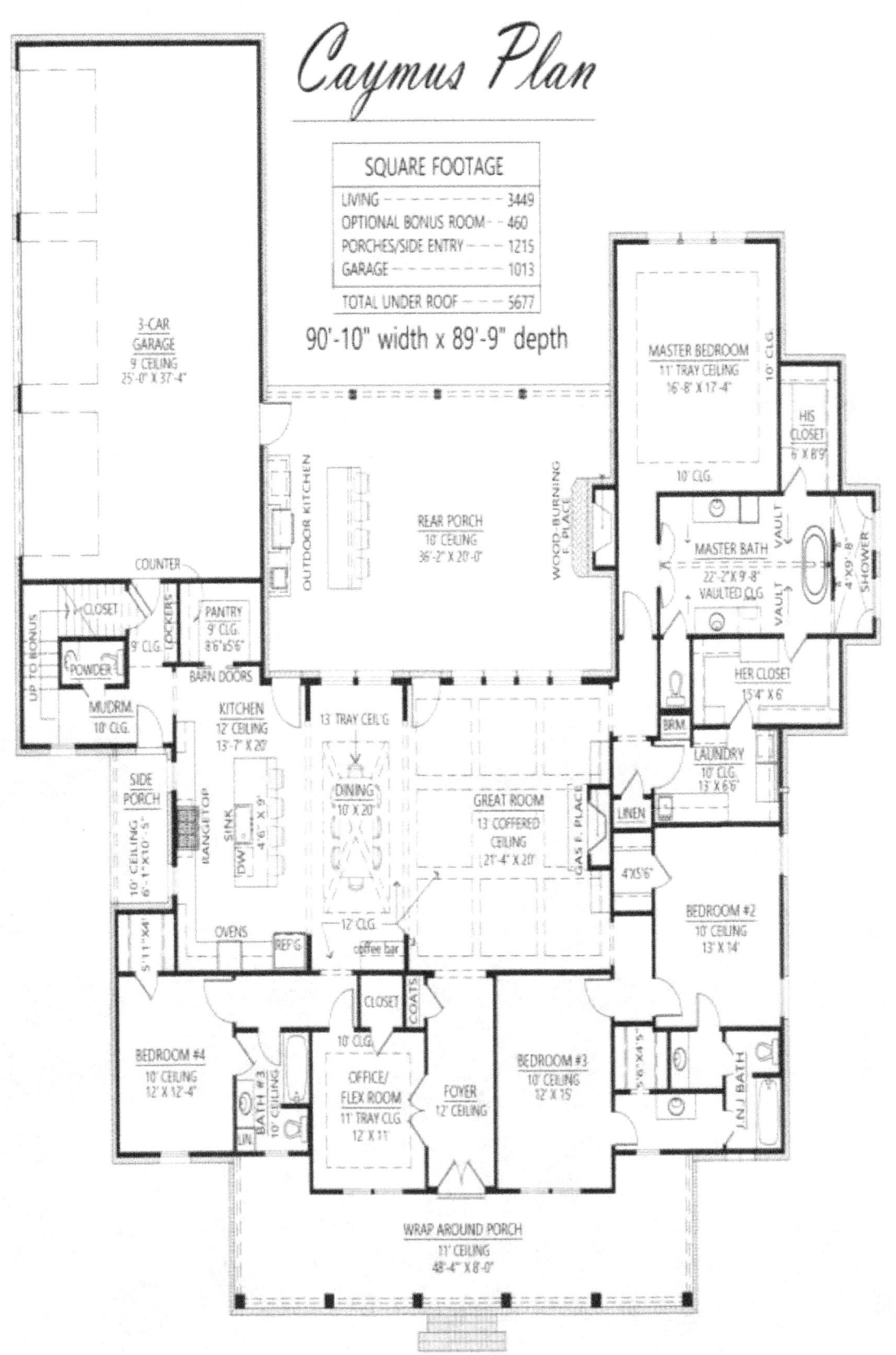

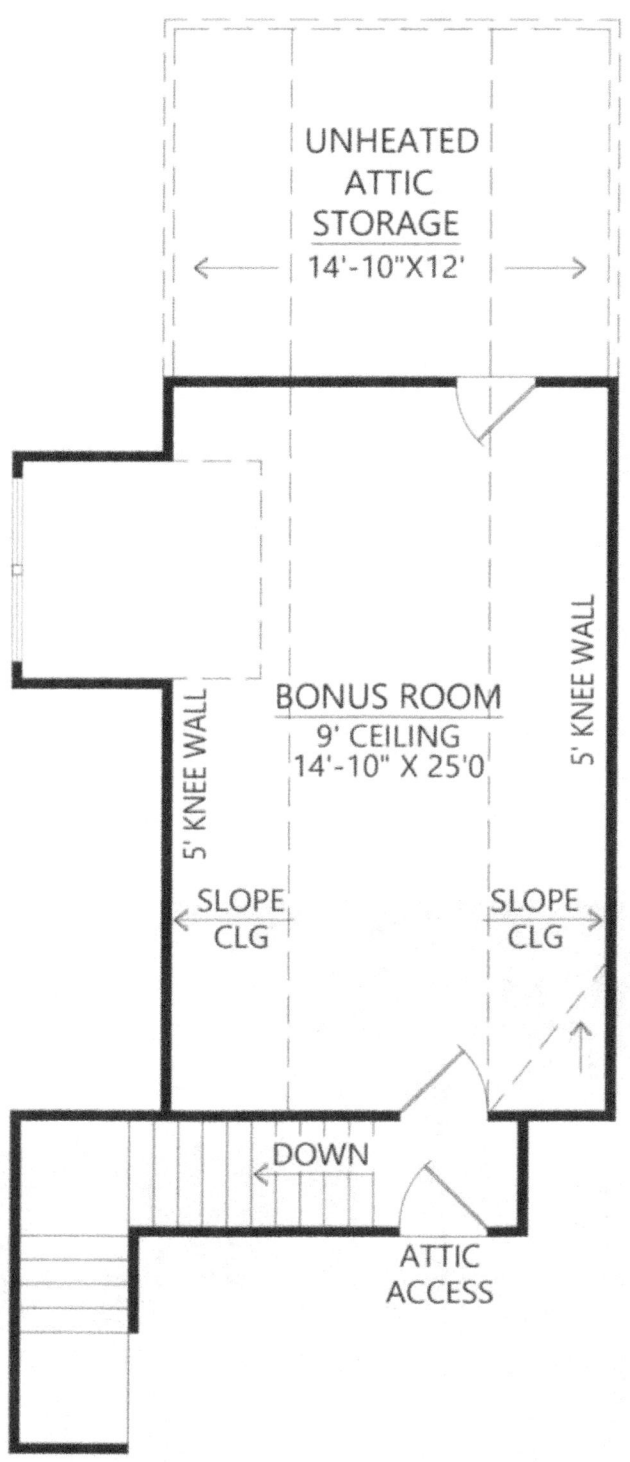

CHAPTER SEVENTEEN: The Windsor Creek Farmhouse Floor Plans

House Plan Features

- Bedrooms: 4
- Bathrooms: 2.5
- Garage Bays: 5
- Main Ceiling Height: 10'
- Main Roof Pitch: 9 on 12

Plan Details in Square Footage

- Living Square Feet: 2326
- Total Square Feet: 4389
- Porch Square Feet: 794
- Garage Square Feet: 587
- Bonus Room Square Feet: 605

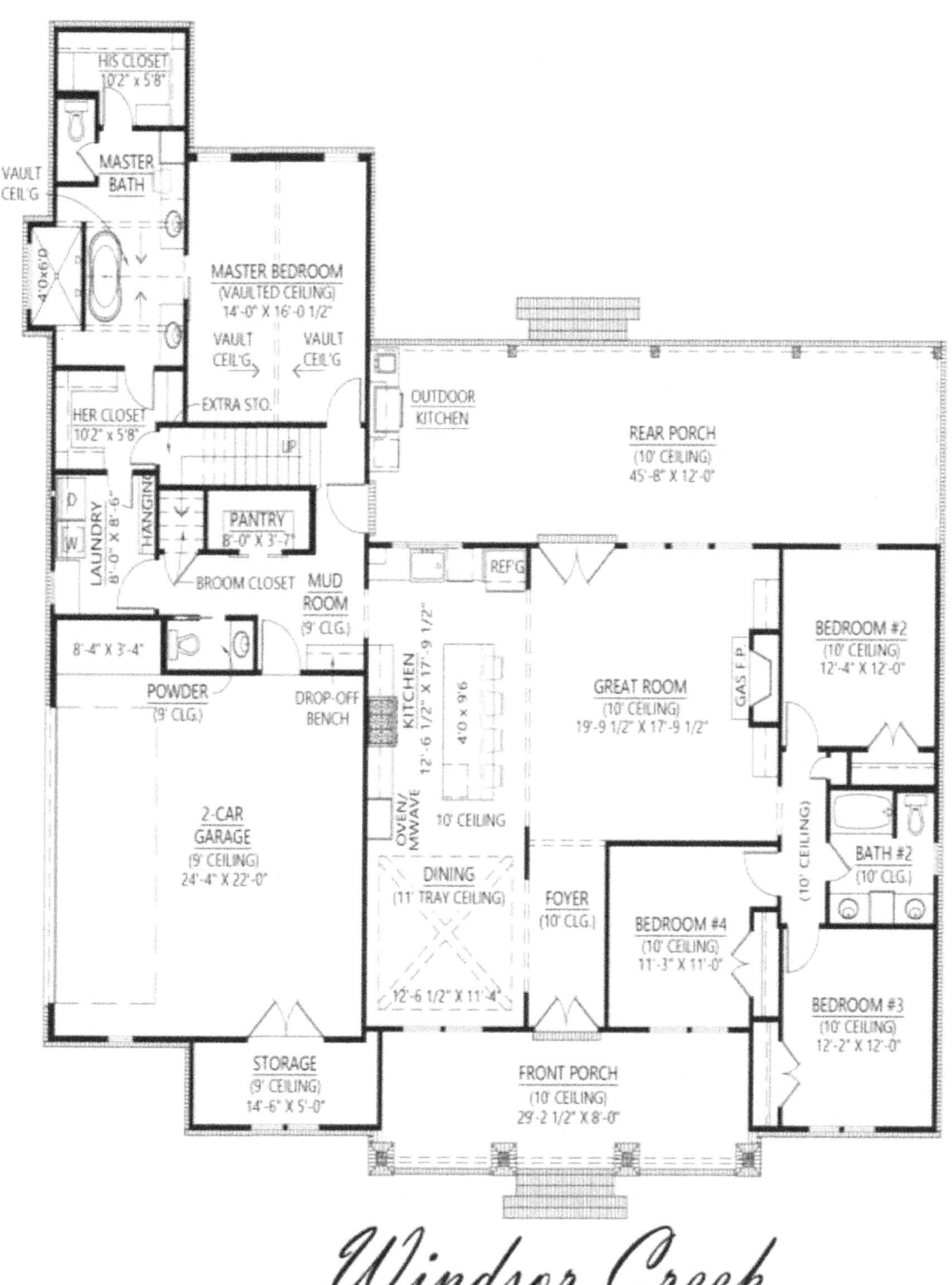

Windsor Creek

72'-10" width x 69'-10 1/2" depth
4 BDRM / 2 1/2 BATH

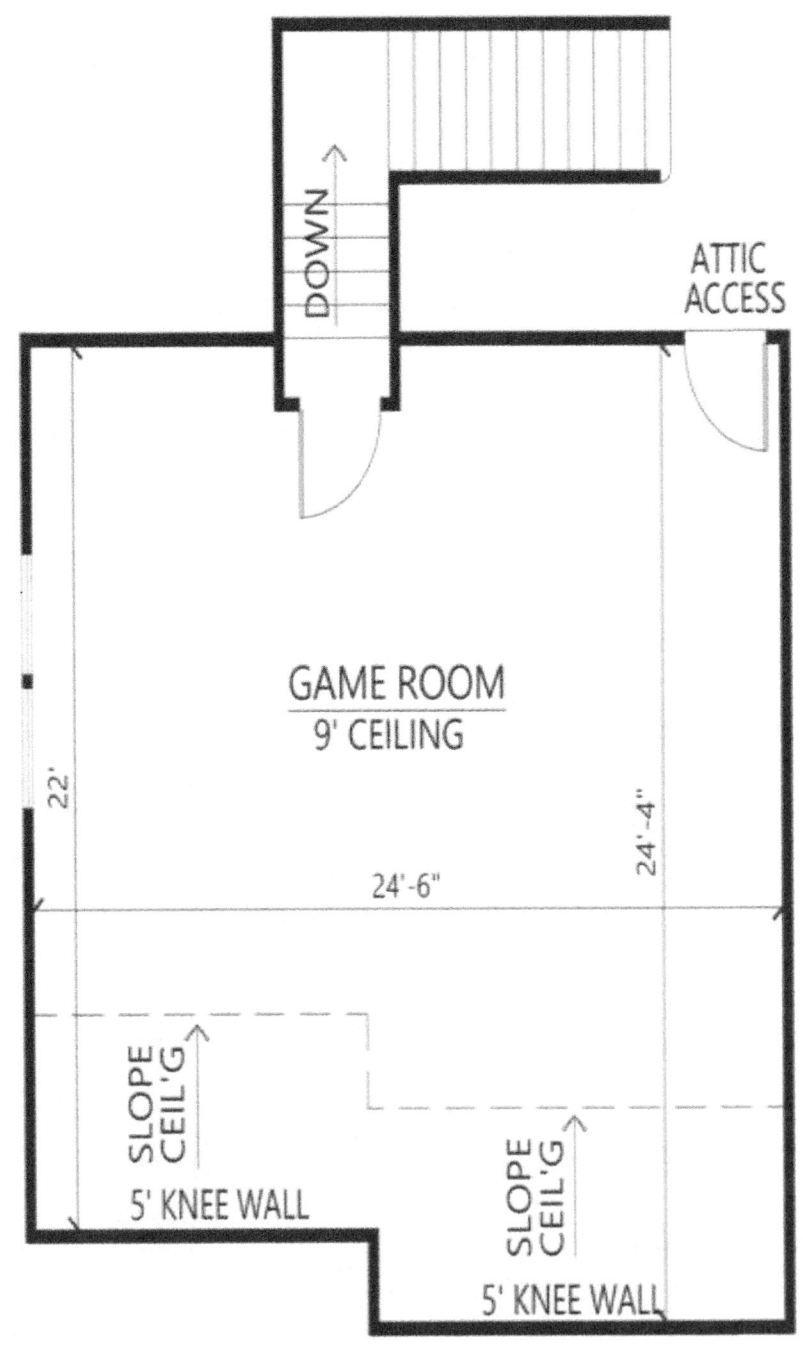

BONUS ROOM

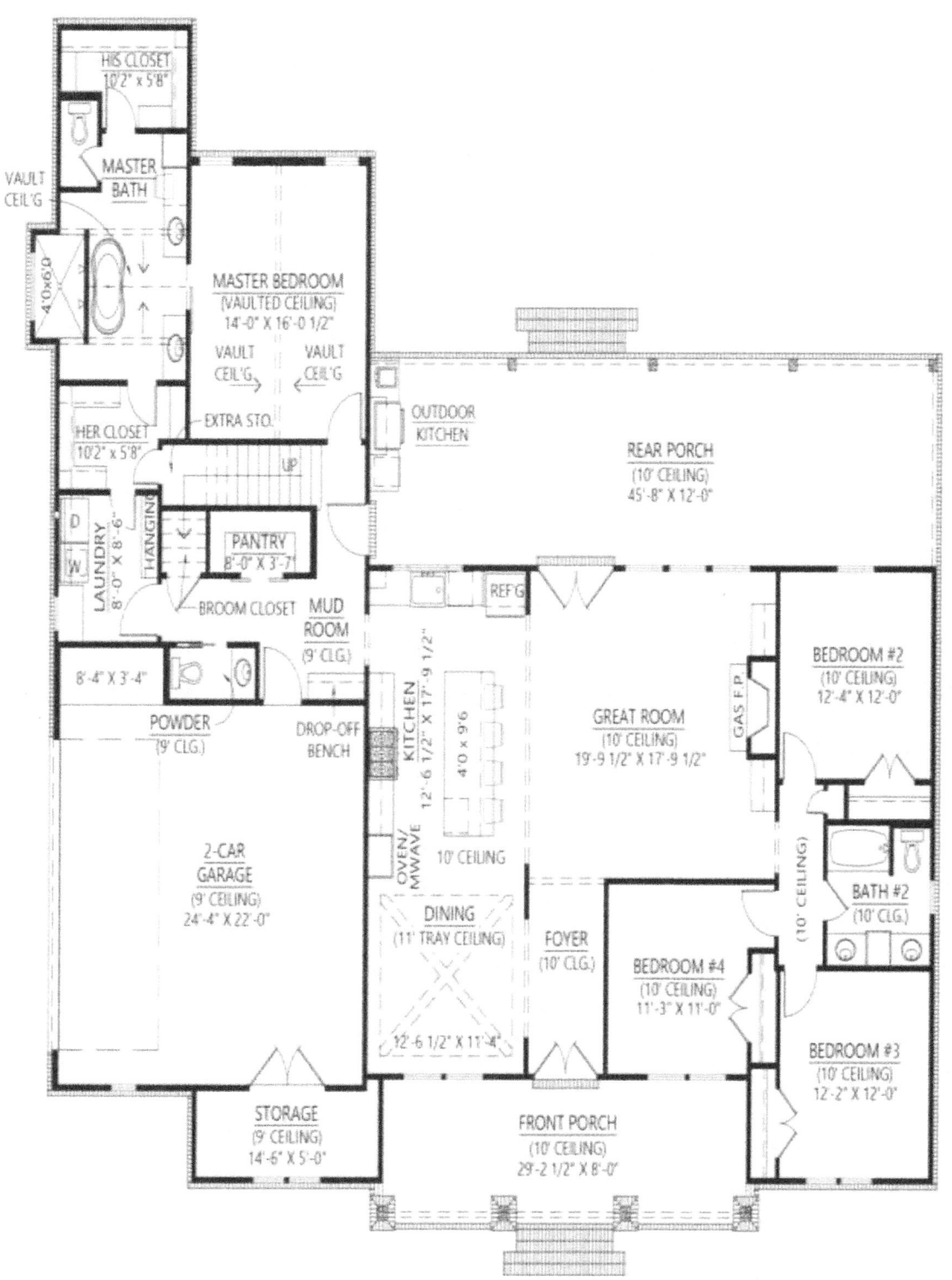

CHAPTER EIGHTEEN: The Valley View Farmhouse Floor Plans

House Plan Features

- Bedrooms: 4
- Bathrooms: 3
- Garage Bays: 2
- Main Ceiling Height: 10'
- Main Roof Pitch: 9 on 12

Plan Details in Square Footage

- Living Square Feet: 2705
- Total Square Feet: 4329
- Porch Square Feet: 986
- Garage Square Feet: 637

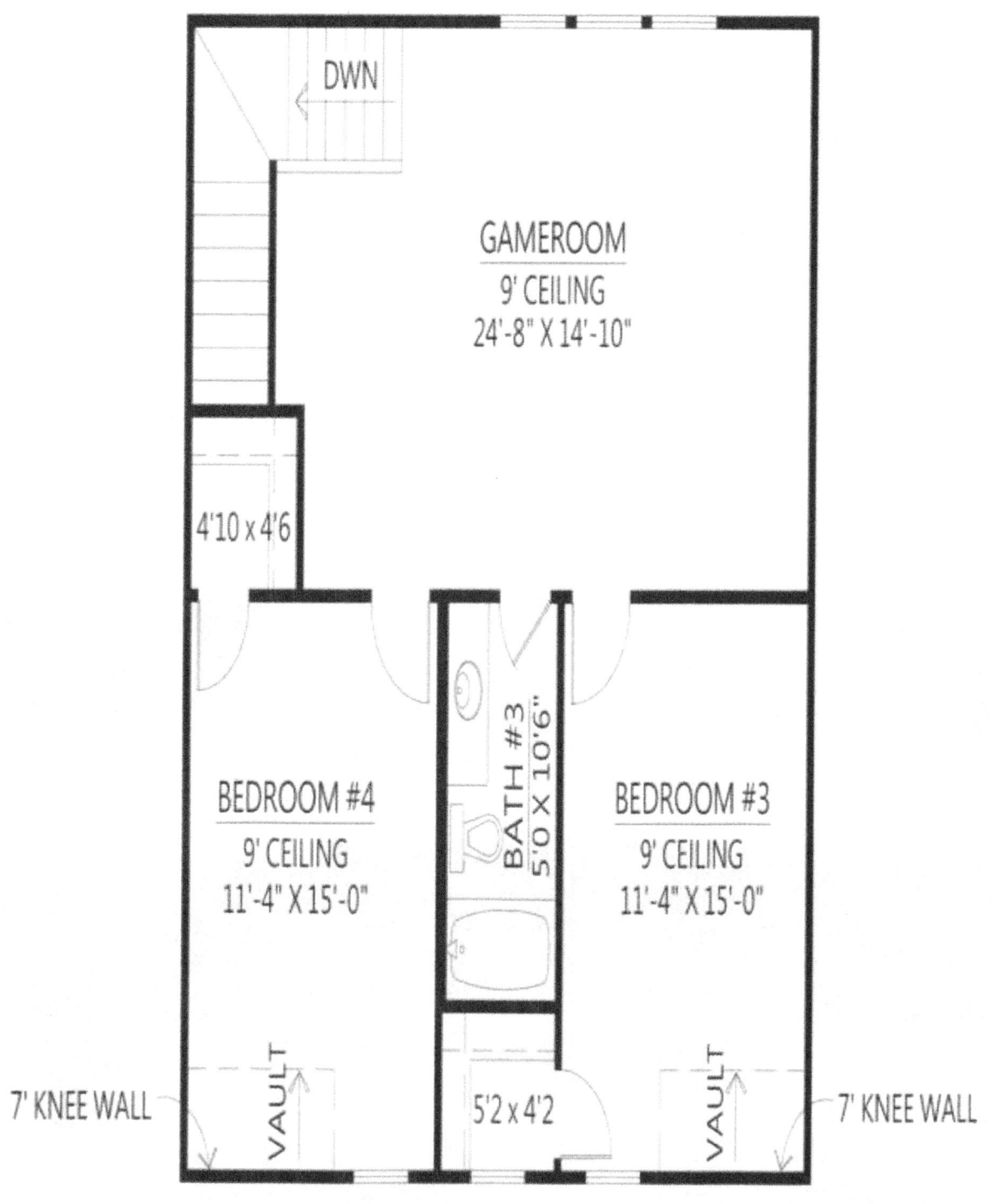

CHAPTER NINETEEN: The Daisey Farmhouse floor plans

House Plan Features

- Bedrooms: 3
- Bathrooms: 2.5
- Garage Bays: 2
- Main Ceiling Height: 9'
- Main Roof Pitch: 8 on 12

Plan Details in Square Footage

- Living Square Feet: 1650
- Total Square Feet: 2708
- Porch Square Feet: 488
- Garage Square Feet: 535

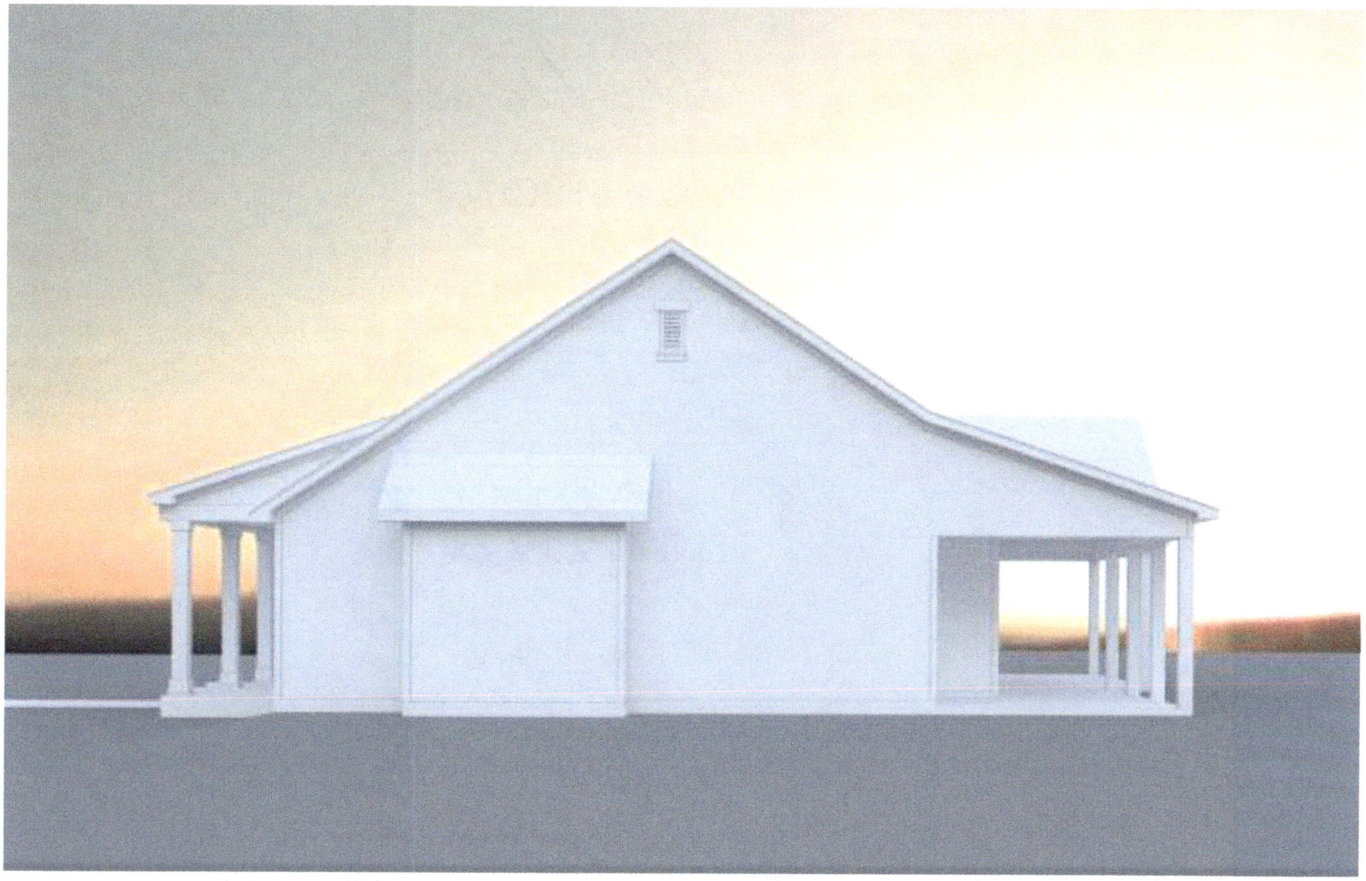

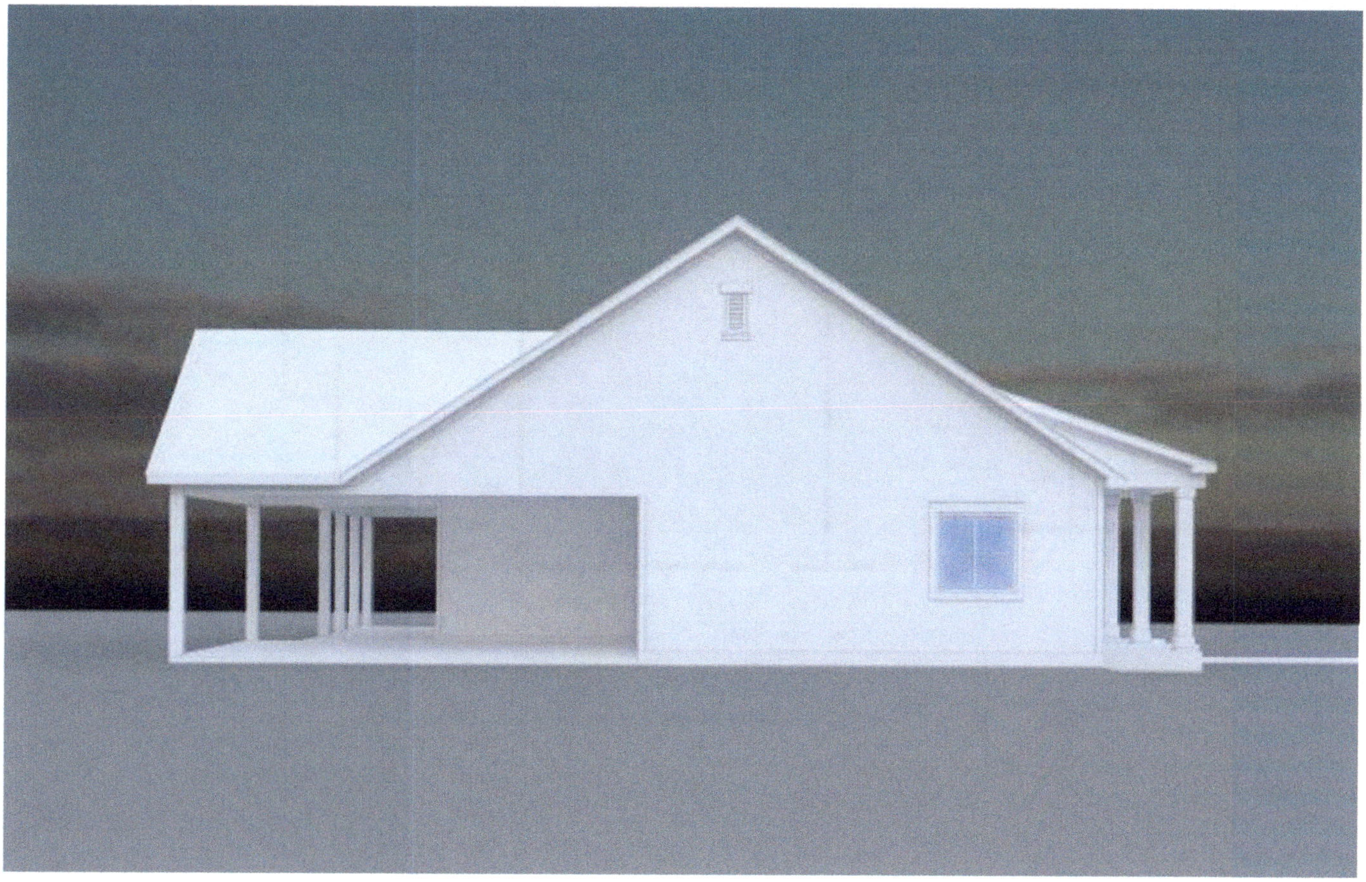

The Daisey

SQUARE FOOTAGE	
LIVING	1650
PORCHES	488
CARPORT	533
STORAGE	35
TOTAL UNDER ROOF	2706

58'-1" width x 54'-4" depth
3 BDRM / 2 1/2 BATH

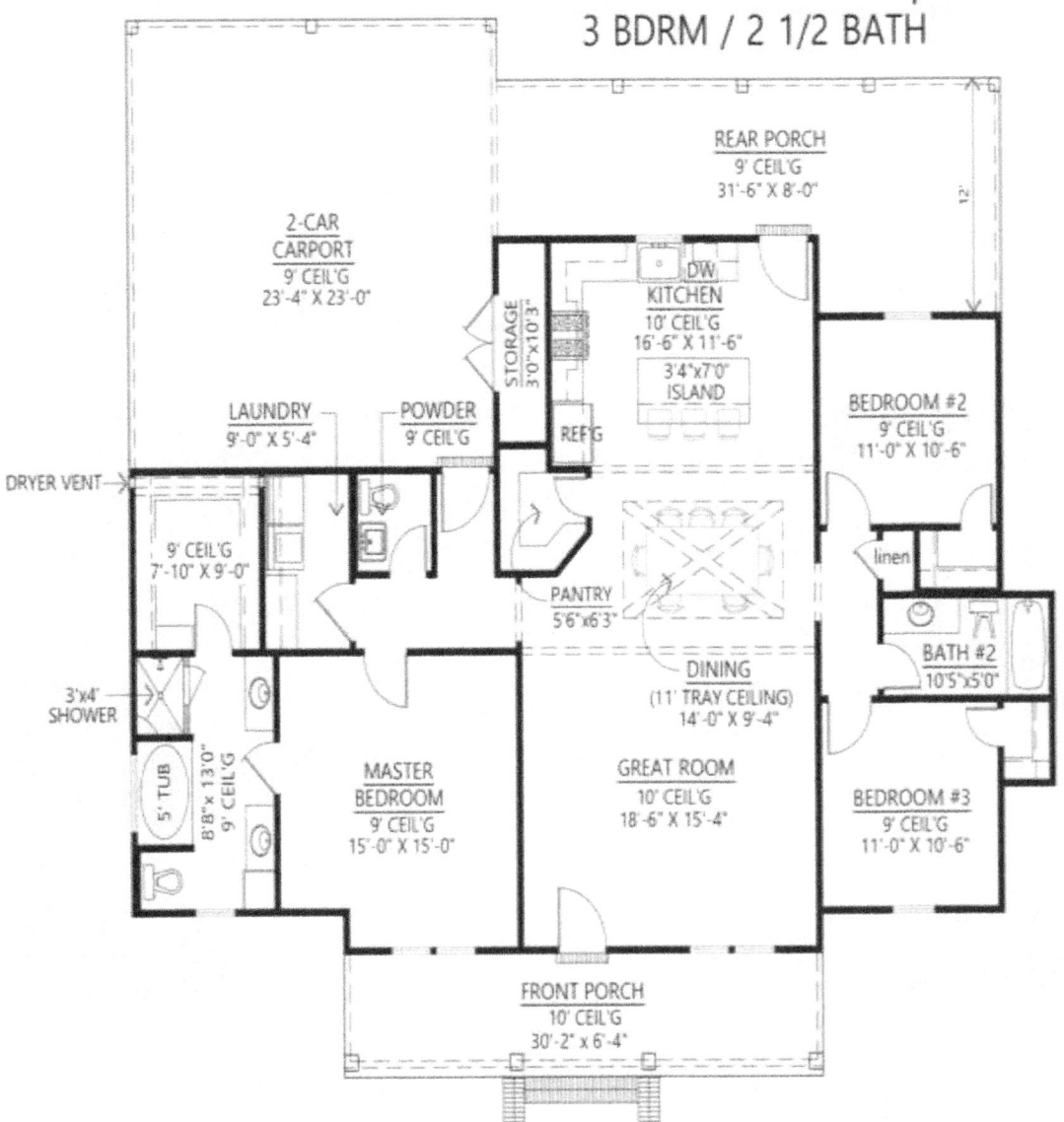

CHAPTER TWENTY: The Merry Oaks Farmhouse Floor plans

House Plan Features

- Bedrooms: 3
- Bathrooms: 2
- Garage Bays: 2
- Main Ceiling Height: 9'
- Main Roof Pitch: 8 on 12

Plan Details in Square Footage

- Living Square Feet: 1676
- Total Square Feet: 2584
- Porch Square Feet: 392
- Garage Square Feet: 519

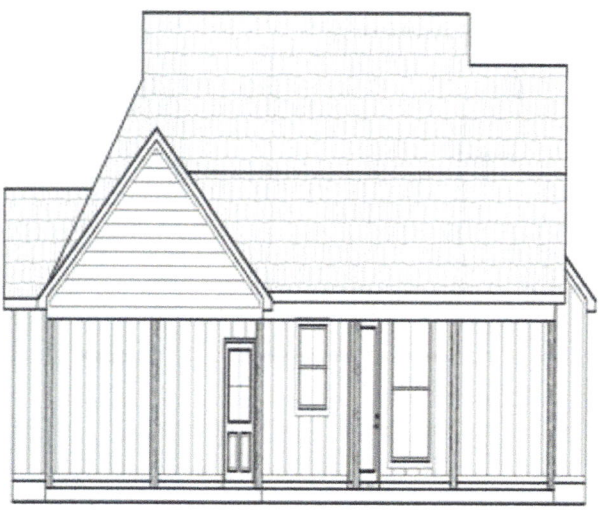

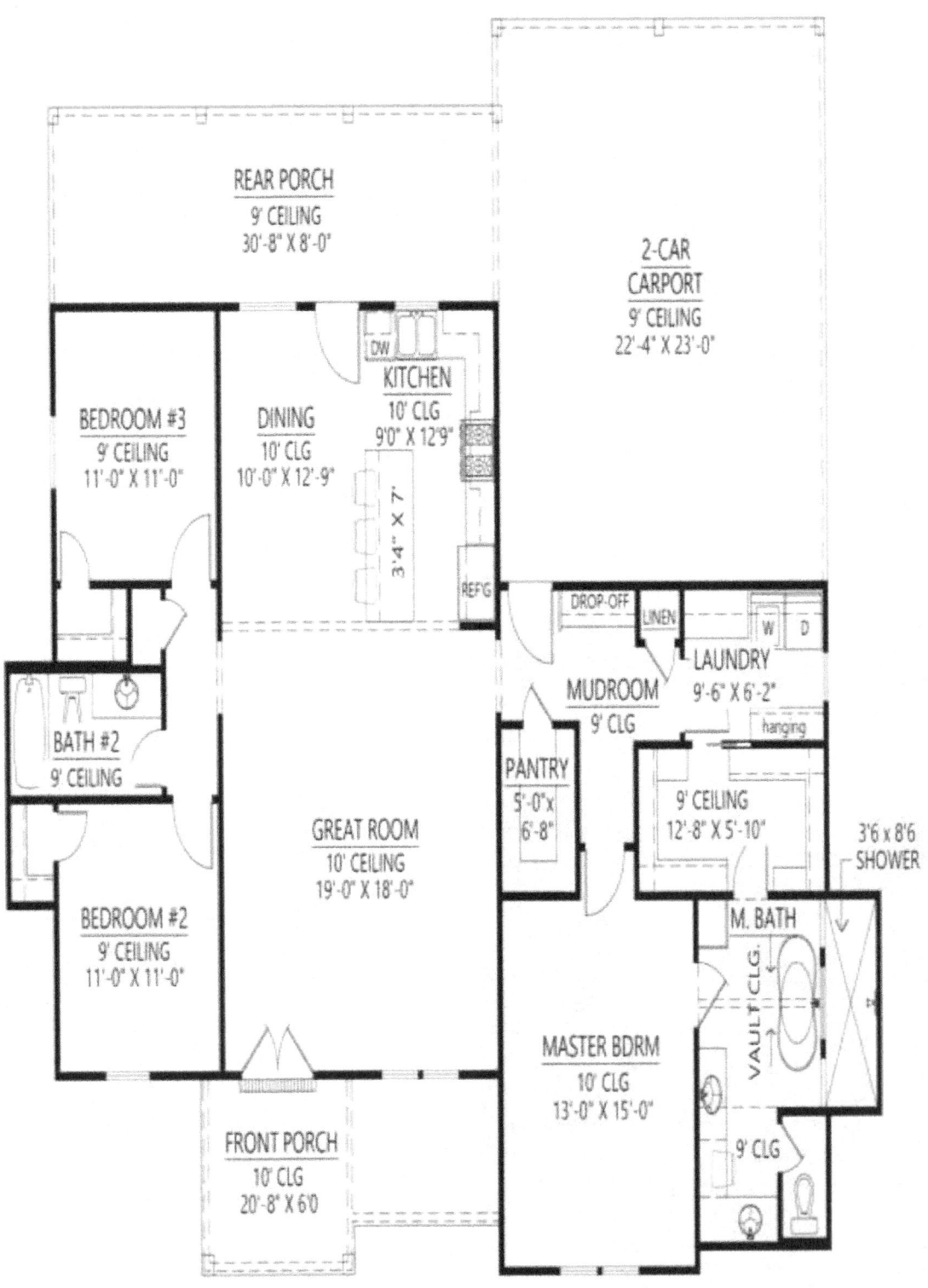

CHAPTER TWENTY-ONE: The Spring Bluff Farmhouse floor plan

House Plan Features

- Bedrooms: 4
- Bathrooms: 3
- Garage Bays: 5
- Main Ceiling Height: 10'
- Main Roof Pitch: 9 on 12

Plan Details in Square Footage

- Living Square Feet: 2147
- Total Square Feet: 3838
- Porch Square Feet: 774
- Garage Square Feet: 579
- Bonus Room Square Feet: 339

Spring Bluff

67'-5" width x 65'-10" depth
4 BDRM / 3 BATH

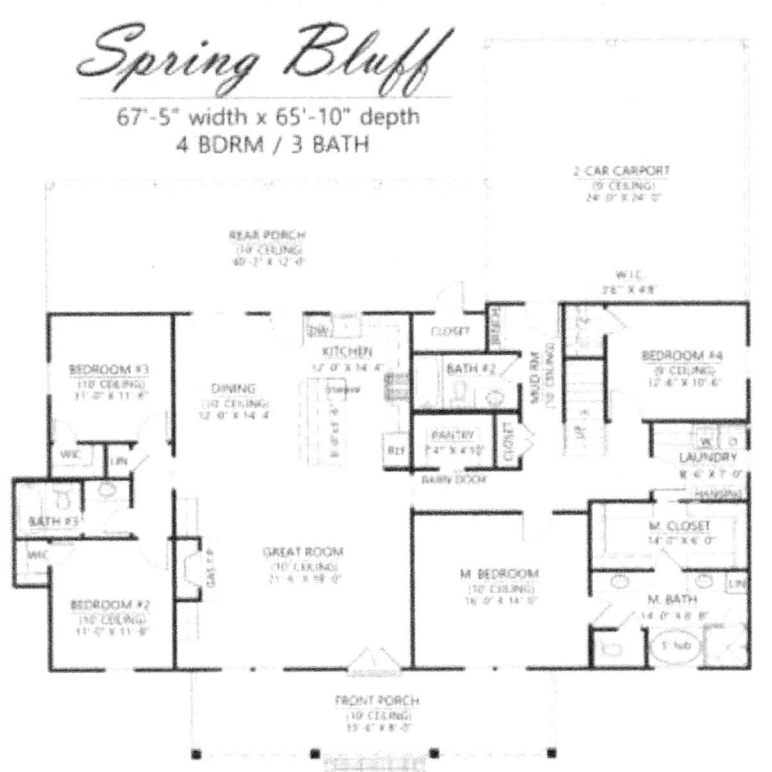
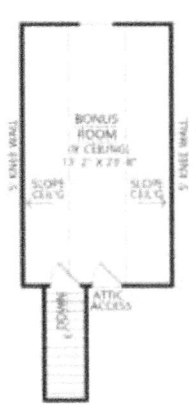

SQUARE FOOTAGE	
LIVING	2147
OPTIONAL BONUS ROOM	339
PORCHES	774
CARPORT	576
TOTAL UNDER ROOF	3836

CHAPTER TWENTY-TWO: The Blackberry Farmhouse floor plan

House Plan Features

- Bedrooms: 3
- Bathrooms: 2.5
- Garage Bays: 2
- Main Ceiling Height: 9'
- Main Roof Pitch: 9 on 12

Plan Details in Square Footage

- Living Square Feet: 1735
- Total Square Feet: 2751
- Porch Square Feet: 487
- Garage Square Feet: 531

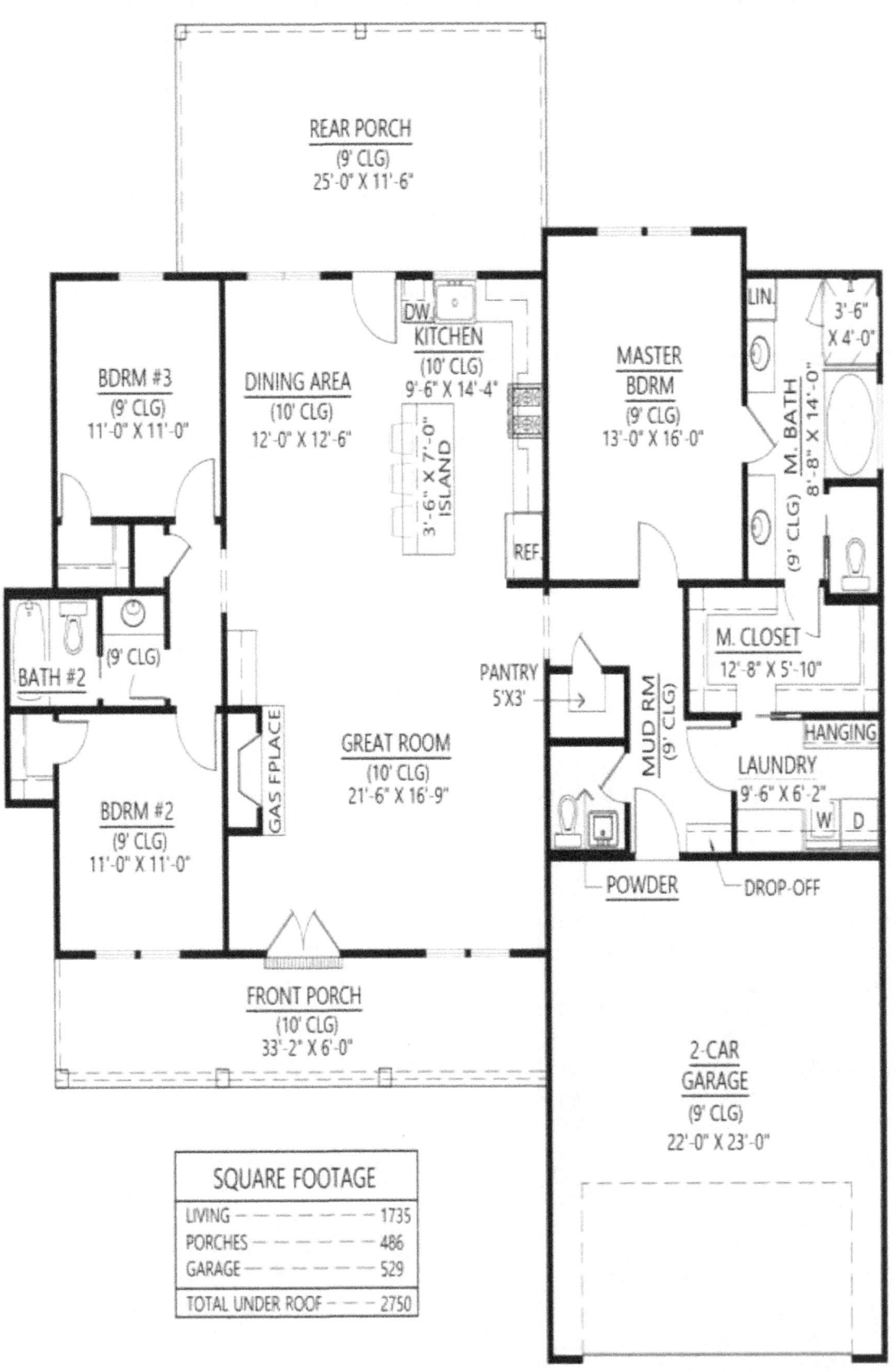

CHAPTER TWENTY-THREE: The Honeysuckle Farmhouse floor plan

House Plan Features

- Bedrooms: 3
- Bathrooms: 2.5
- Garage Bays: 2
- Main Ceiling Height: 10'
- Main Roof Pitch: 9 on 12

Plan Details in Square Footage

- Living Square Feet: 1924
- Total Square Feet: 3179
- Porch Square Feet: 681
- Garage Square Feet: 574

Honeysuckle farmhouse

3 BDRM / 2 1/2 BATH

SQUARE FOOTAGE	
LIVING	1924
PORCHES	681
GARAGE	574
TOTAL UNDER ROOF	3179

61'-7" width x 61'-8" depth

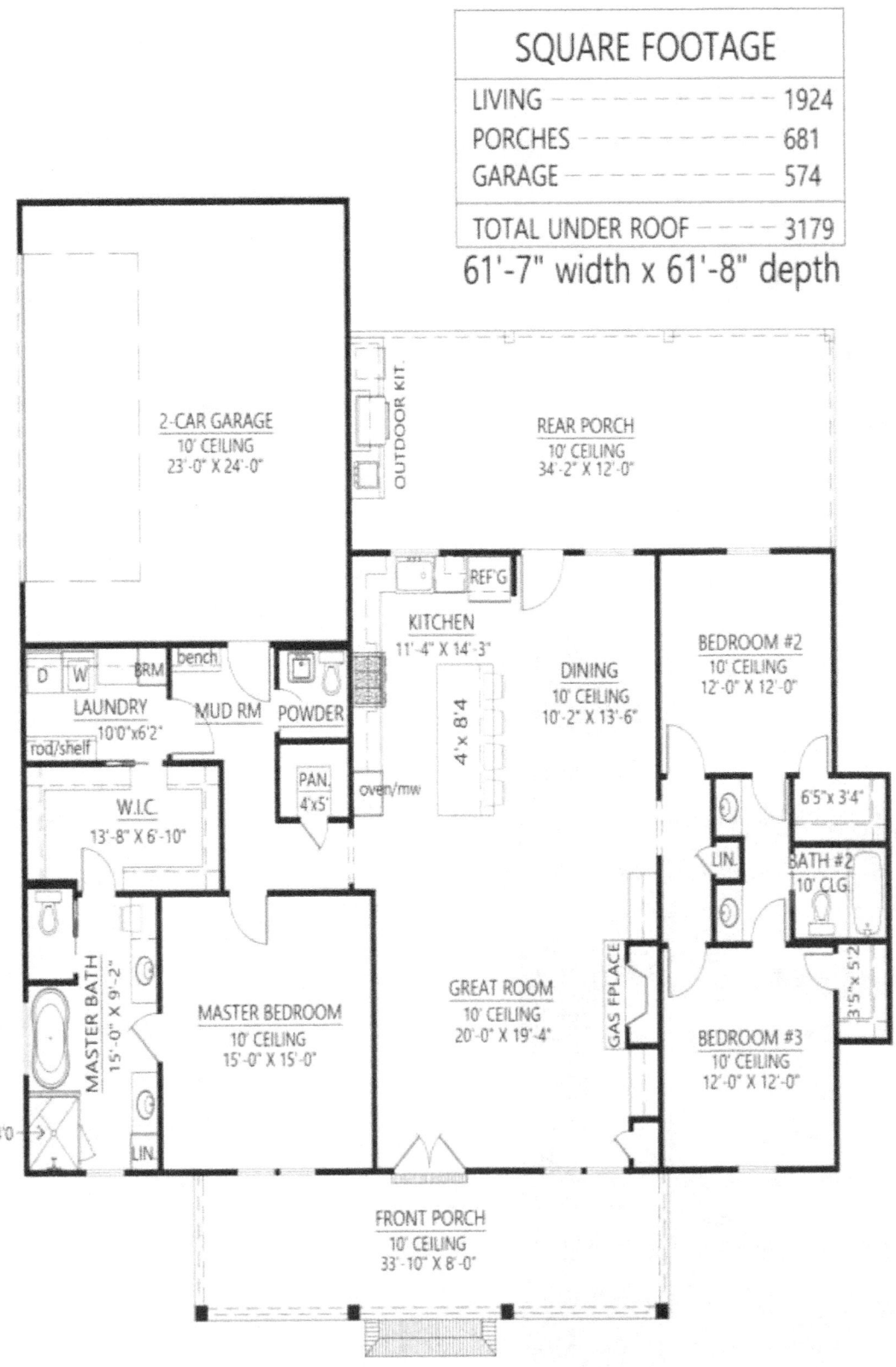

CHAPTER TWENTY-FOUR: The Mulberry Farmhouse floor plans

House Plan Features

- Bedrooms: 3
- Bathrooms: 2

Plan Details in Square Footage

- Living Square Feet: 1817
- Total Square Feet: 2874
- Porch Square Feet: 448
- Garage Square Feet: 609

CHAPTER TWENTY-FIVE: The Aspen Hill

House Plan Features

- Bedrooms: 3
- Bathrooms: 2.5

Plan Details in Square Footage

- Living Square Feet: 2230
- Total Square Feet: 4229
- Porch Square Feet: 760
- Garage Square Feet: 568
- Bonus Room Square Feet: 414

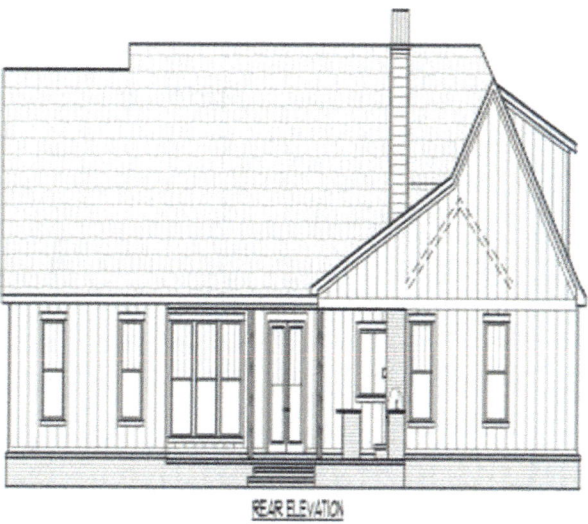

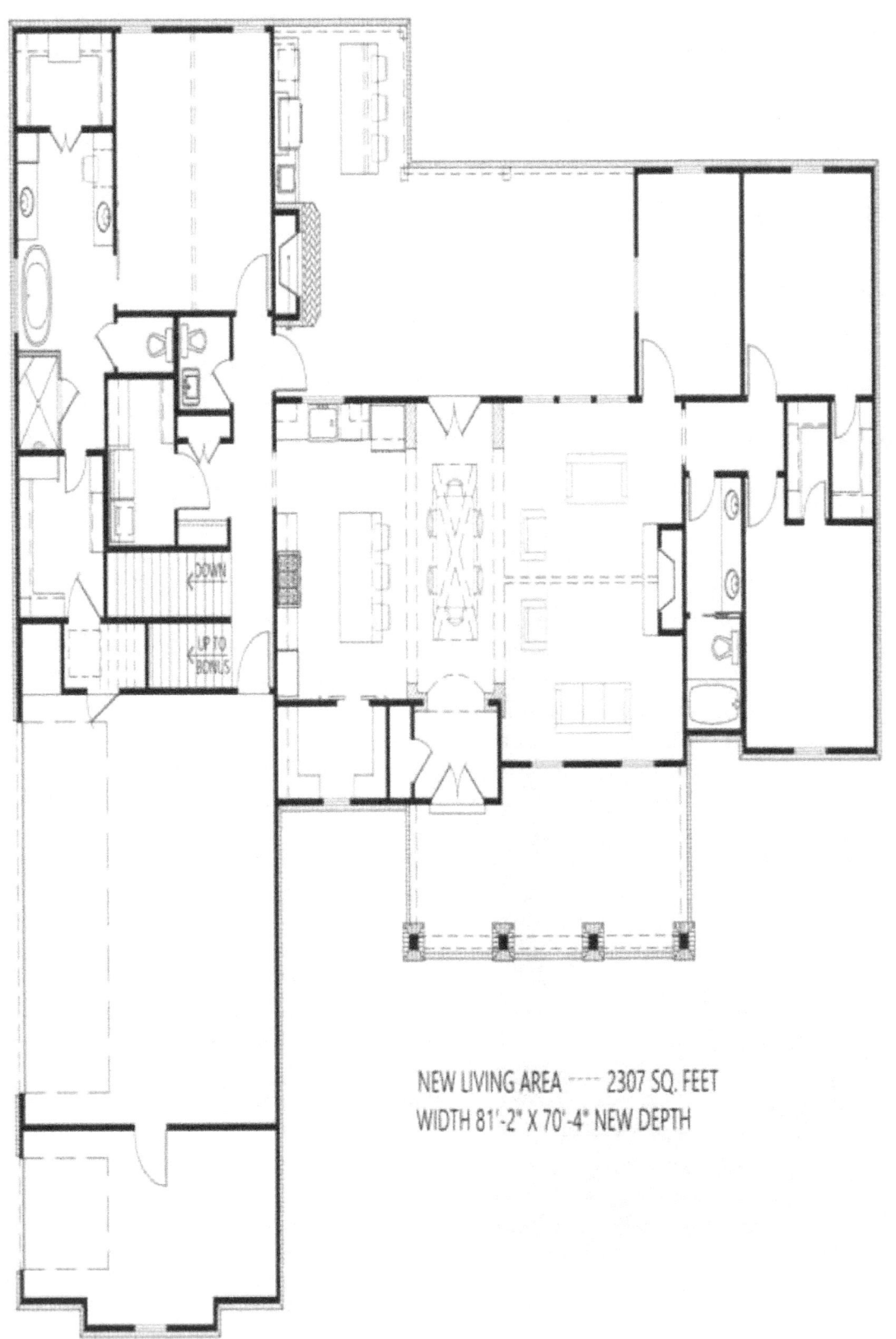

NEW LIVING AREA ---- 2307 SQ. FEET
WIDTH 81'-2" X 70'-4" NEW DEPTH

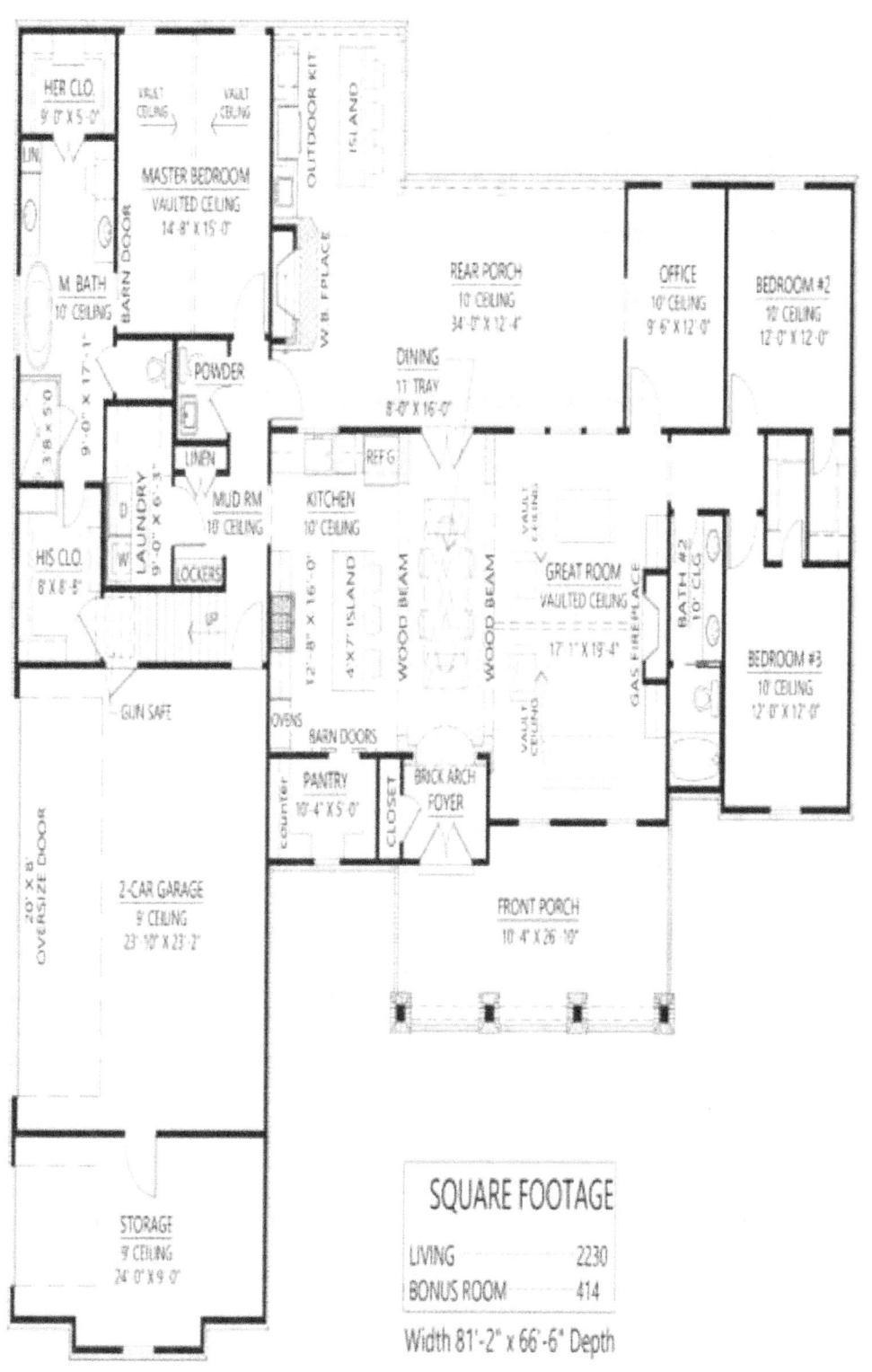

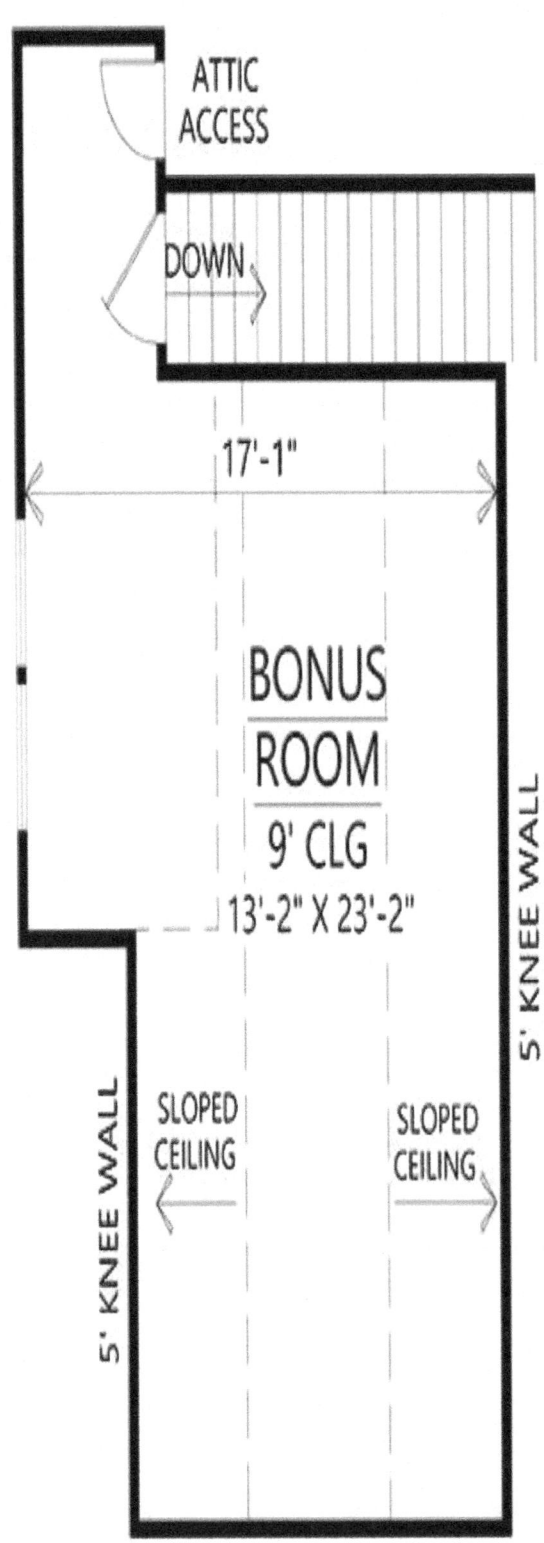

CHAPTER TWENTY-SIX: The Saddletree Farmhouse Floor plan

House Plan Features

- Bedrooms: 4
- Bathrooms: 3.5

Plan Details in Square Footage

- Living Square Feet: 2035
- Total Square Feet: 3164
- Porch Square Feet: 573
- Garage Square Feet: 556
- Bonus Room Square Feet: 1

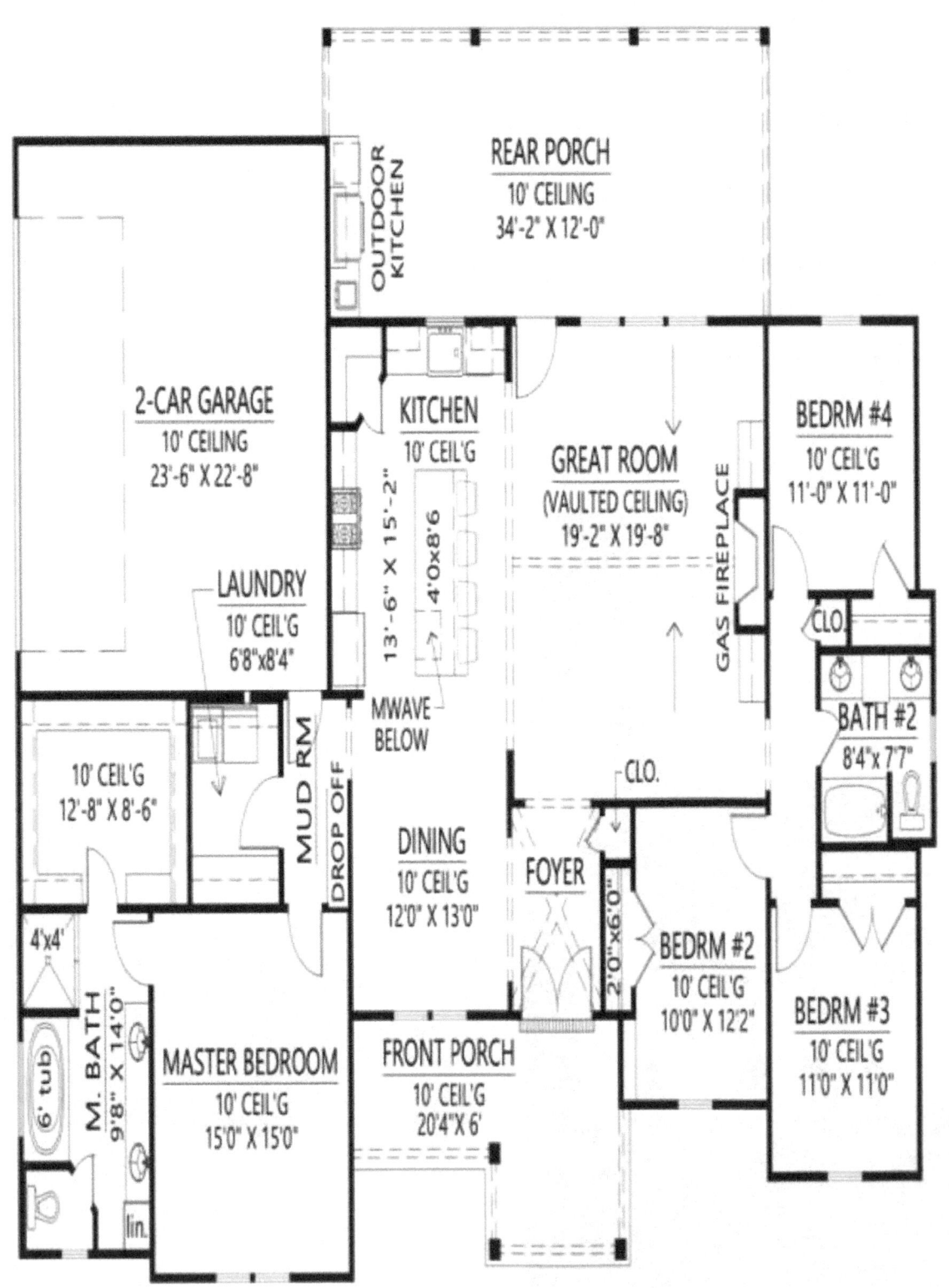

CHAPTER TWENTY-SEVEN: The Indian Trail Farmhouse floor plan

House Plan Features

- Bedrooms: 4
- Bathrooms: 2.5

Plan Details in Square Footage

- Living Square Feet: 2234
- Total Square Feet: 3382
- Porch Square Feet: 492
- Garage Square Feet: 624

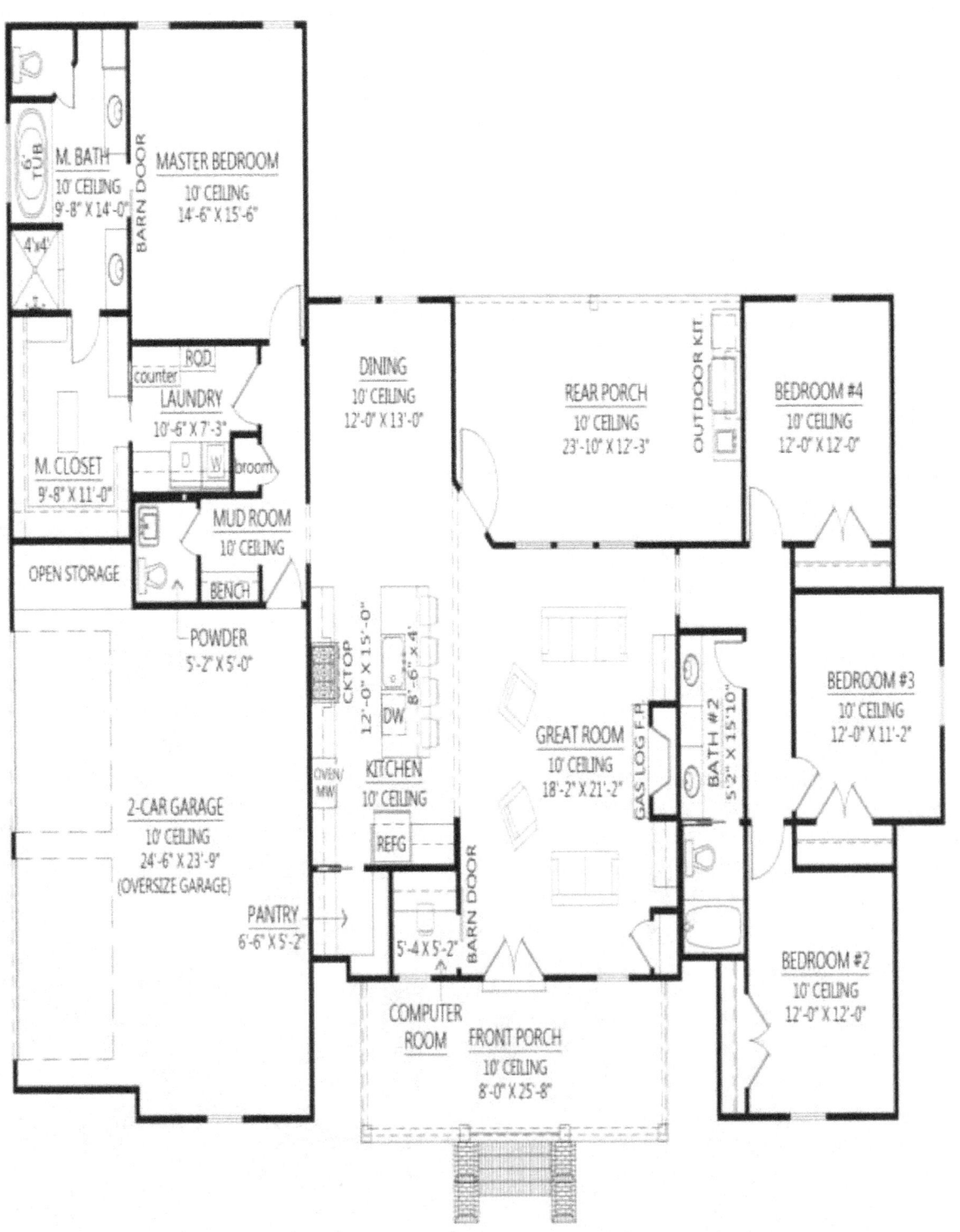

CHAPTER TWENTY-EIGHT: The Sandy Ridge Farmhouse floor plan

House Plan Features

- Bedrooms: 4
- Bathrooms: 3
- Main Roof Pitch: 9 on 12

Plan Details in Square Footage

- Living Square Feet: 3175
- Total Square Feet: 5076
- Porch Square Feet: 931
- Garage Square Feet: 970

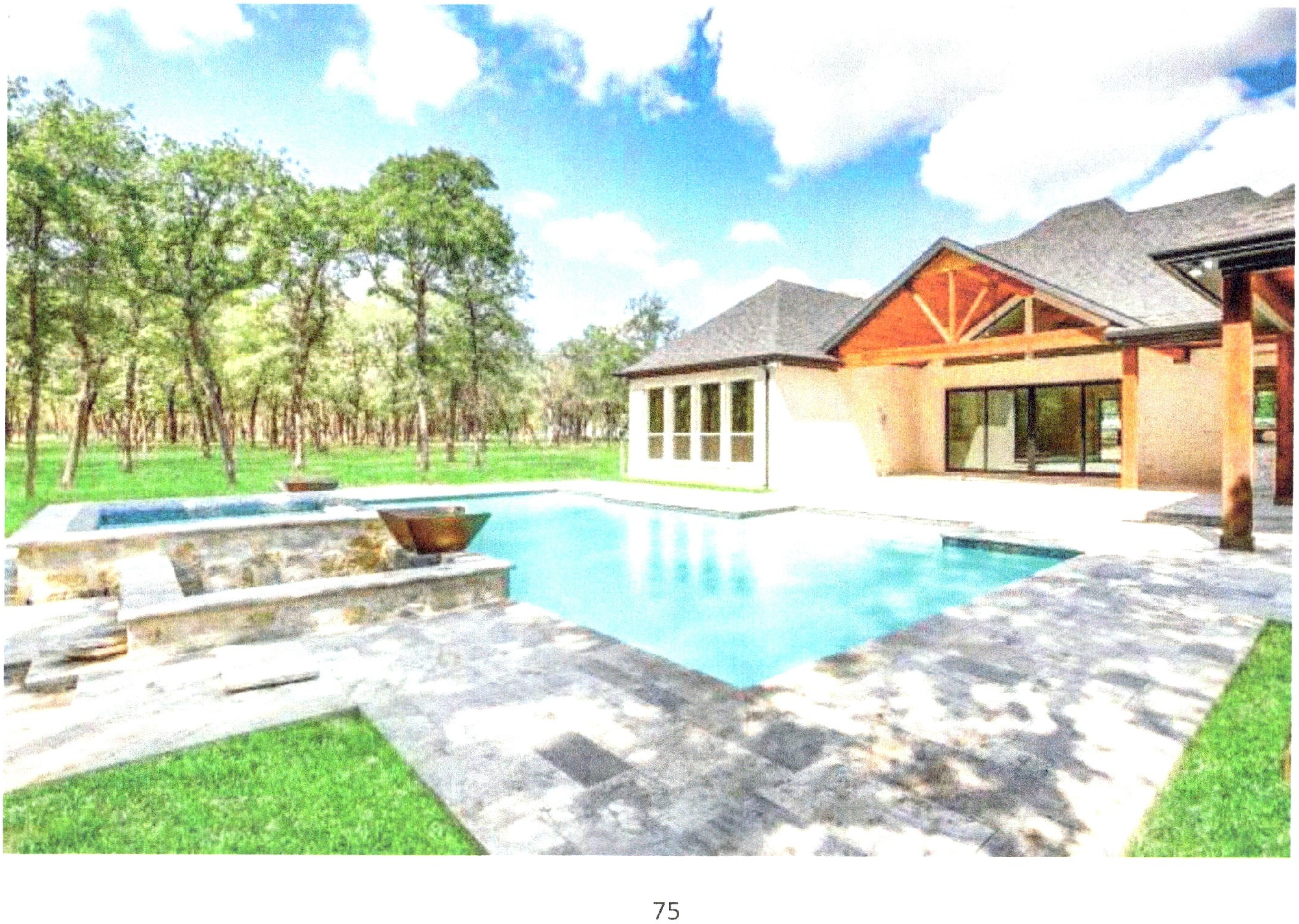

75

Sandy Ridge

SQUARE FOOTAGE	
LIVING	3175
FRONT PORCH	268
REAR PORCH	663
GARAGE	970
TOTAL SQ. FT.	5076

Width 92'-3" x 73'-8" Depth

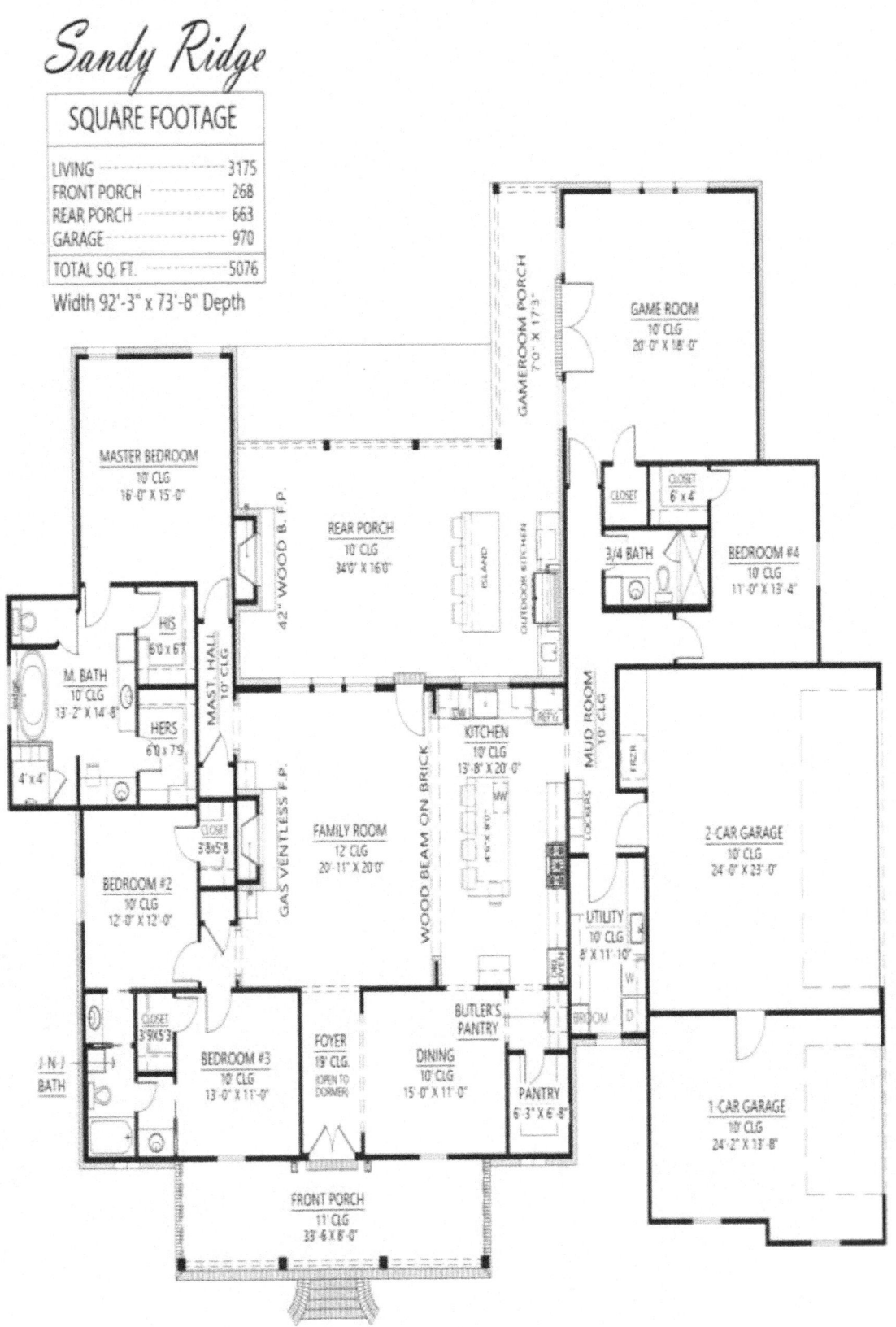

CHAPTER TWENTY-NINE: The Cherry Grove Farmhouse floor plan

House Plan Features

- Bedrooms: 4
- Bathrooms: 2
- Main Roof Pitch: 9 on 12

Plan Details in Square Footage

- Living Square Feet: 2342
- Total Square Feet: 3625
- Porch Square Feet: 790
- Bonus Room Square Feet: 433

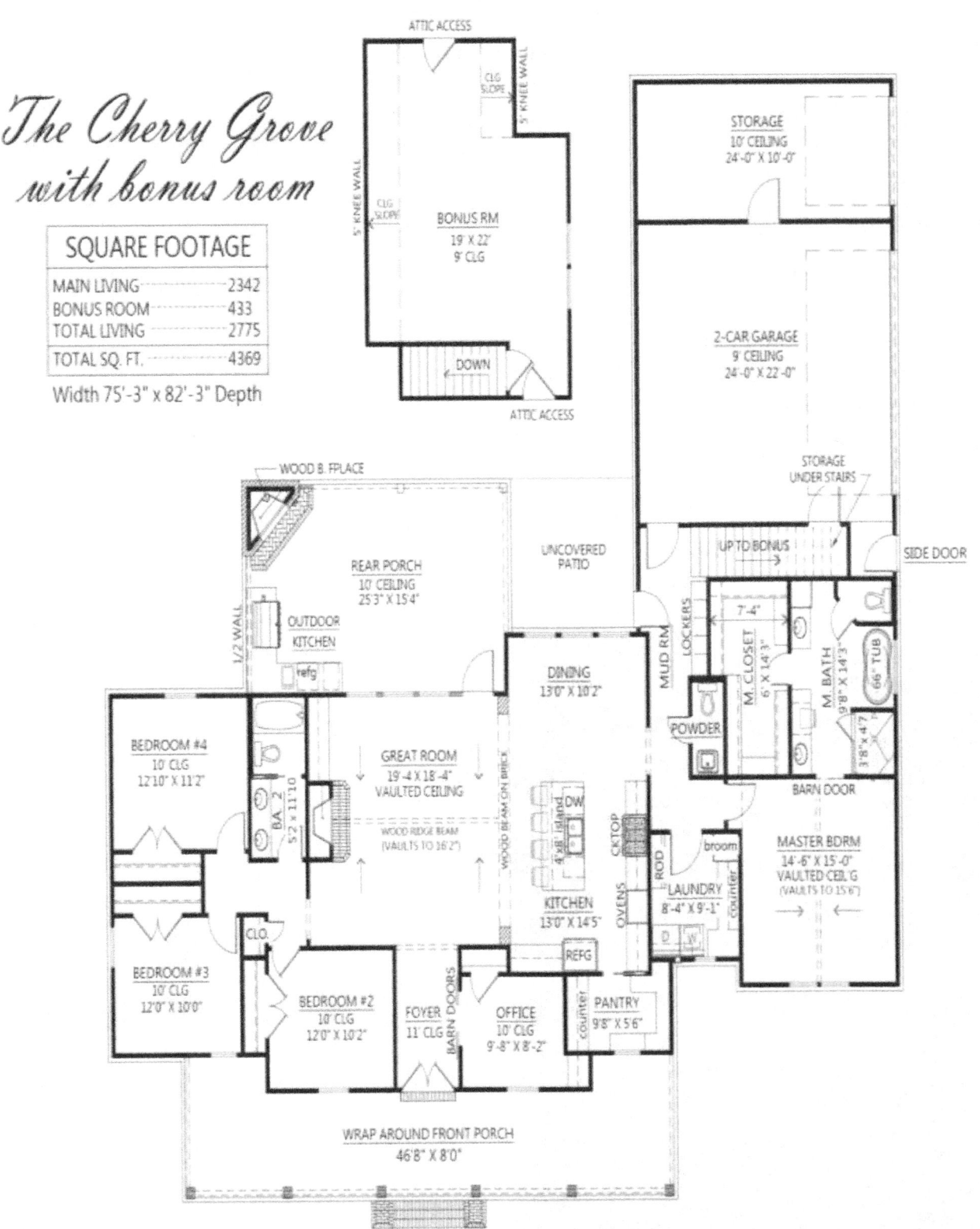

The Cherry Grove

SQUARE FOOTAGE

LIVING — 2232
TOTAL SQ. FT. — 3622

Width 75'-3" x 70'-8" Depth

CHAPTER THIRTY: The Cotton Grove Farmhouse floor plan

House Plan Features

- Bedrooms: 4
- Bathrooms: 3
- Main Ceiling Height: 10'
- Main Roof Pitch: 9 on 12

Plan Details in Square Footage

- Living Square Feet: 2716
- Total Square Feet: 4415
- Porch Square Feet: 691
- Garage Square Feet: 919
- Bonus Room Square Feet: 522

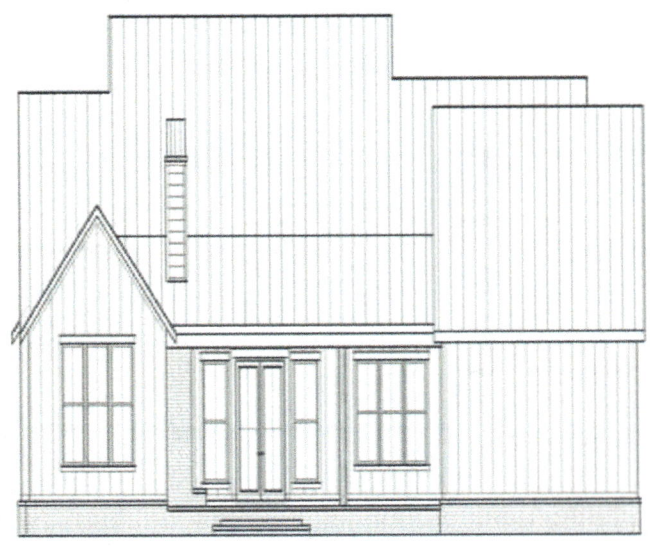

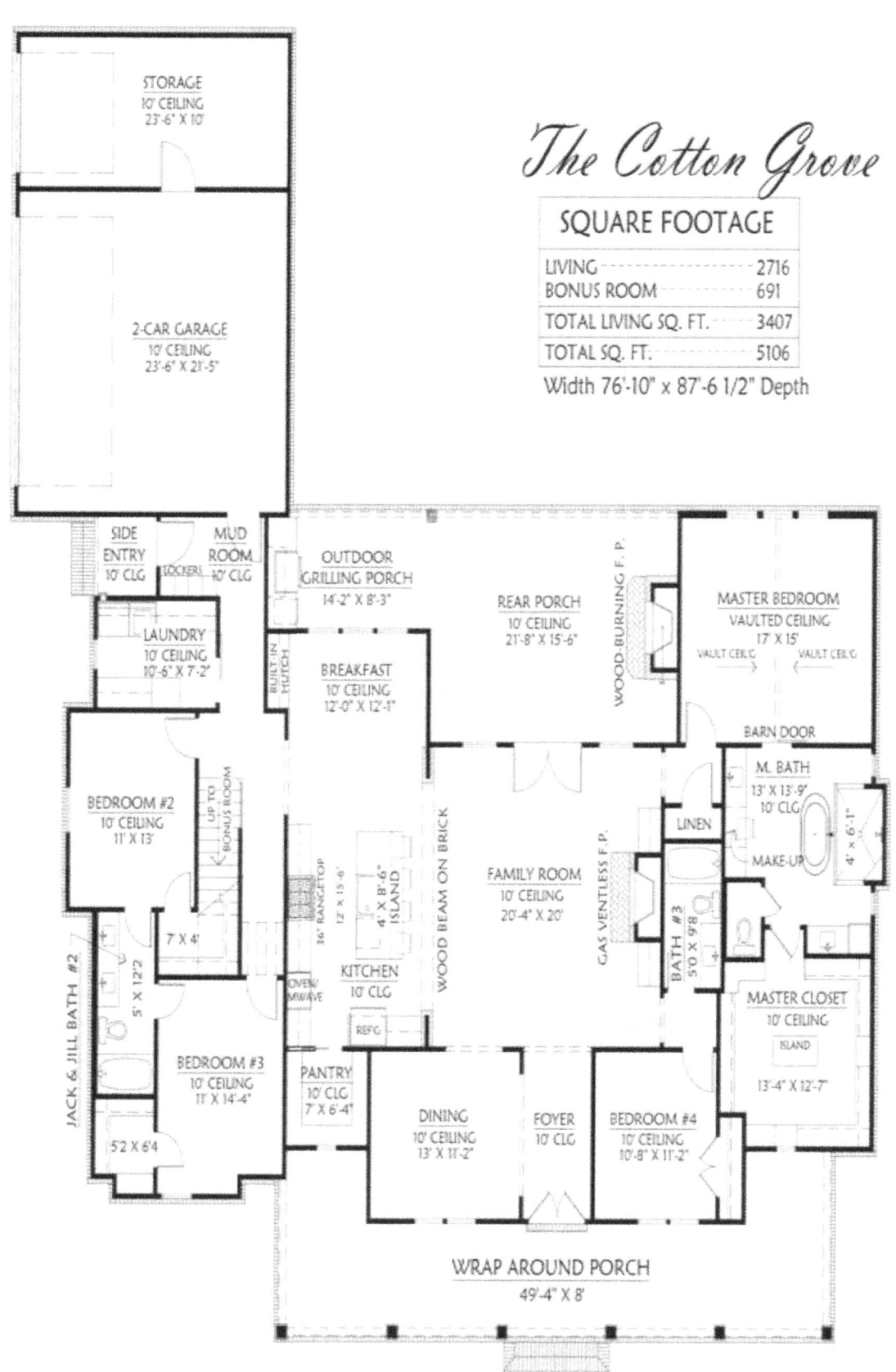

The Cotton Grove

SQUARE FOOTAGE

LIVING	2716
BONUS ROOM	691
TOTAL LIVING SQ. FT.	3407
TOTAL SQ. FT.	5106

Width 76'-10" x 87'-6 1/2" Depth

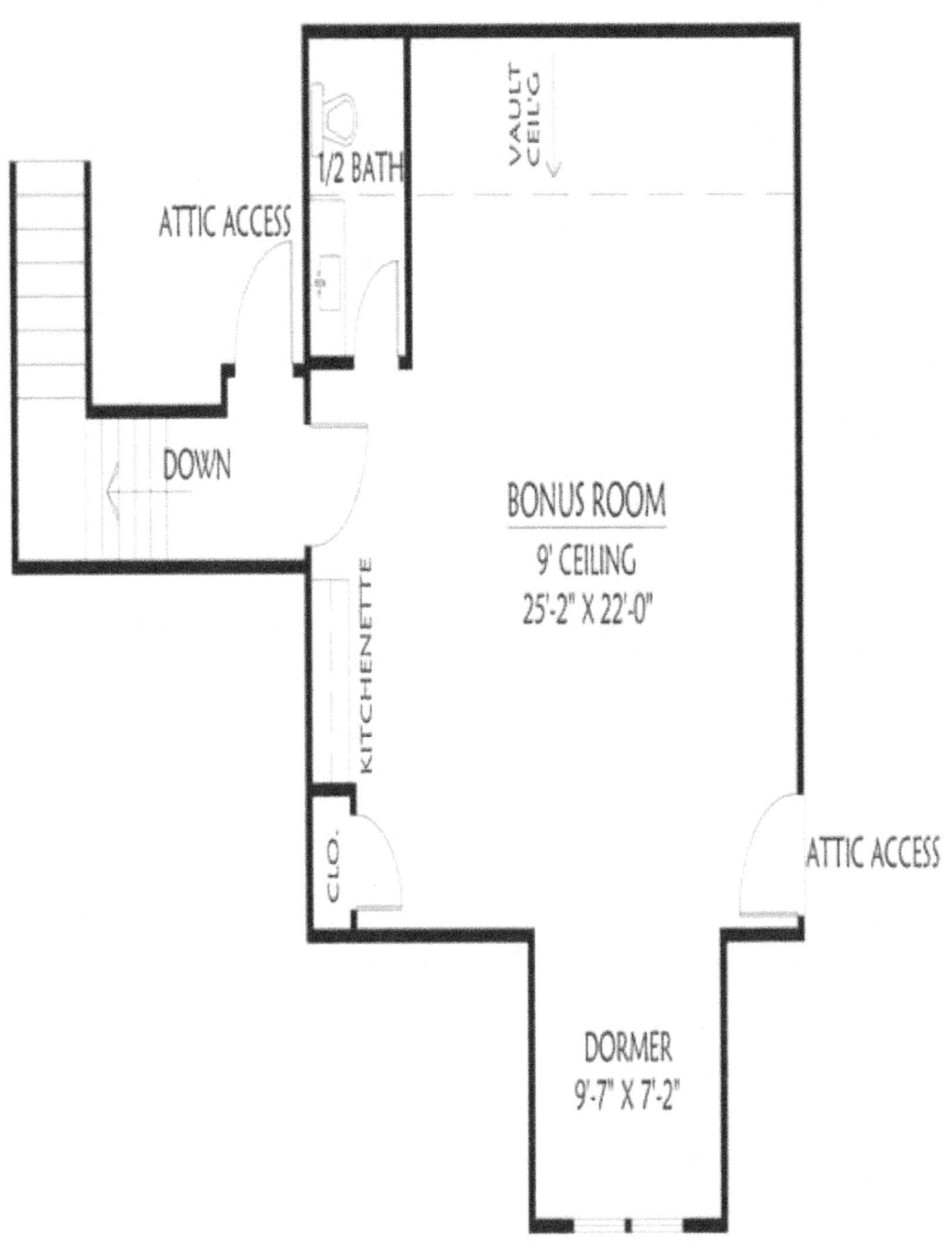

Made in the USA
Monee, IL
06 September 2023

42231825R00050